T0083448

This Body That Inhabits Me

THE ITALIAN LIST

This Body That Inhabits Me

ROSSANA ROSSANDA

EDITED WITH AN AFTERWORD BY
LEA MELANDRI

TRANSLATED BY RICHARD BRAUDE

LONDON NEW YORK CALCUTTA

The Italian List
SERIES EDITOR: Alberto Toscano

Seagull Books, 2022

First published in Italian as *Questo corpo che mi abita*
by Rossana Rossanda
© Bollati Boringhieri editore, Turin, 2018

First published in English translation by Seagull Books, 2022
English Translation © Richard Braude, 2022

ISBN   978 0 8574 2 903 2

British Library Cataloguing-in-Publication Data
A catalogue record for this book is available from
the British Library

Typeset by Seagull Books, Calcutta, India
Printed and bound in the USA by Integrated Books International

CONTENTS

1

Self-Defence of a Political I

21

A Hussar Called Hope

38

Théroigne de Méricourt:
Neither Commoner nor Lady

47

Depth and History

61

On the Threshold of Mystery

75

Raise the Red Lantern

81

This Body That Inhabits Me

98

Afterword
Friendship, a Calm Deposit of Self
LEA MELANDRI

120

Index of Names

1

SELF-DEFENCE OF A POLITICAL I*

No reader of my book—a collection of articles written over more than a decade[1]—has been more loving than Lea.[2] No one remained so close. No one wrote to me so lovingly to say: 'Oh unhappy soul, you are wrong.'

Here lies a first difference between us. I find it difficult to read Lea's work—and this was true even before I knew her—without feeling that we are riding 'different waves' and that she is therefore wrong. I have thought much about how she sees me, a vision that also reflects her own way of being, and I think it rests on another way of establishing the 'I', of establishing interiority. I do not know if this makes her happy, and I am

---

* First published in *Lapis. Percorsi della riflessione femminile*, 1 November 1987.

1 Rossana Rossanda, *Anche per me. Donna, persona, memoria dal 1973 al 1986* (Milan: Feltrinelli, 1987).

2 Lea Melandri, 'Una vita scritta a molti', *il manifesto*, 15 March 1987.

not wont to measure those fundamental choices by which a person constructs themselves in terms of the level of happiness it might bring them. I am interested in who she is, how she reflects and accepts or rejects me, how she makes me think; I like that she likes me while shaking her head as if standing in front of a battle lost in advance. Yet she need not be concerned for me. Not because I am a fully developed, wise and happy beast—quite on the contrary. But because it does not make much sense to say to a woman of my age, shape, background and occupation: 'She still hasn't found her independence, she's martyred herself for that same old female dependence—and while others are directly dependent on man, for her this has simply become a dependence on man's universe, on his public commandments.' For the Left also lays down commandments, Lea is quite right about that. Yet saying this would be futile, not because it is too late but because this is who I am, and it would be—shall we say it?— affectionately authoritarian to claim: 'Given that a woman must exist first and foremost for herself, in the end she cannot live as Rossana does.' Ever since I've been involved in politics—that is, almost my entire life—I too have felt the imperious desire to say to the other, 'But you should be different!' And, for the same length of time, I have nevertheless hesitated in saying to myself, 'If I tell him this then I'll free him, I'll point him towards a happier path.' 'Perhaps,' I always wonder, 'I should ask something of myself first.' A life is a life. You can take heed of mine or otherwise, but there is no need to waste time lamenting it. I have constructed it, and not everyone can say the same of themselves: indeed, very few—because very few have had our (perhaps tortuous) freedom to do so. It is an autonomous journey, in the strict sense that I have given myself my own law, and it does not make much sense to object to me by saying: 'You only think that you have done so.' This game can continue ad infinitum, but *we* won't. Yes, the axis of my life is the relation with the other, but I reject the claim that this is synonymous with dependence. I would be more inclined to say that the choice of establishing the self on the basis of oneself is autistic, an escape from the reality principle. A kind of dream. If my own is a dream—because relating oneself to that which is outside of us is always the construction of a projection, a project, a question, a risk—then non-relating is simply a different kind of dream; perhaps, of the two, the latter is nourished by greater fantasy. But perhaps I'm wrong. What matters is that I don't care to define an autonomy based on myself alone. I know no such thing, it doesn't interest me much, in the same way that the conceptual abstraction of the autonomy of 'female humankind'[3] does not

3 *Genere umano* is usually translated as 'human species', 'human race' or 'humankind'; while *genere* translates into the English 'gender', as well as 'genre' or 'kind'. The locution *genere umano femminile* evokes the tension between 'gender' and 'humankind at stake' in this discussion. [Trans.]

excite me; it is something quite different from sexual difference, because sexual difference—in my view—is not *a priori* ontological: it is a determining and not totalizing aspect of my existence as a person/woman, in this place and time in a history in which I am contingently located.

This is who I am, and before attempting to explain the far from simple reasons for this, I would like to avoid for anyone to consider me, even by dint of affection, as a martyr; as crucified for others. As far back as I can remember, I came into this world with an immense curiosity to understand myself and the other. Along with an ever-present impossibility of considering myself as belonging to an orbit around which 'the other' gravitates (a person, worldly goods, this present moment in the arc of my existence), I have kept them at a sufficient distance so that I can live without being aware of them and choosing the moments when I draw near to them.

I think of myself as a female unit in a plenum of male and female units[4] each of which sends and receives 'structuring' messages of the self. I think of the 'self', of the I, as a surface that receives, selects, rejects,

4 '*una in un pieno di uni e une*': a formula to which Melandri will also return in her essay later in this volume; it presents a particular problem in translation as it relies on the Italian gendered articles *una* and *un*, and the plural forms *uni* and *une*. Here I have rendered the meaning of the original phrase, if not its elegance. [Trans.]

resends, dialogues, forms itself, informs itself, clashes
and—so long as consciousness endures, so long as *non
occidit brevis lux*[5]—grows like a plant in the earth of the
other, both human and otherwise, the other that surrounds us and lives or sub-lives or breathes or exhales
around us. The other persons or forms of this 'other'
enchant me. I provide them with the dimensions of my
form, a form whose shadowy zones and luminosity I
know as suffering and need; I know how, every day, I
am the 'result' of a different value, and I believe that
others experience the same thing. They enchant me, in
the sense that I live because I enjoy seeing them, touch-
ing them, thinking to myself about this similarity / difference. I have never given up on believing that the
individual cannot be repeated, and I always smile at the
efforts of the stars to drag us towards an 'engraved' destiny from which we flee like meteors, and to which we
return when we do not know how else to provide ourselves with another 'meaning' and how being without
meaning makes us feel dizzy. In these 'others' I have
attempted—as far as one can, because in the end one
can't—to embrace that originality which cannot be
repeated; this unrepeatable originality (which has
always enchanted me) has enchanted me twice in love.
I did not search for the fusion: the perception of the

---

5 A reference to *Catullus 5*, the ode by the Roman poet Catullus
to his lover Lesbia, *occidit brevis lux*, was translated by Thomas
Campion as 'once is set out little light', by Walter Raleigh as
'after our short light'. [Trans.]

beating of another blood, another emotion filled me with a certain tenderness—the moments one searches for, the hand that offers itself, words exchanged. This is always a wager that hangs on the brink of failure, because we remain separated individuals—it is necessary to love oneself in order truly to understand and forgive oneself and the other for the extraordinarily different territory which (neither understood by us nor understanding us) seems to rise up against us, delegitimating us along with our loving gaze. In 'politics' (to use a word that twenty years ago I would not have used because there's politics and then there's politics) it has been the same for me: whether from near or far (though it seems to me we're all connected by more or less perceivable threads), I've seen people who couldn't manage to *be*, trapped as they were by useless unfreedoms. Useless in the sense that they stem from bullying, arrogance, or actions of power that can be condemned and rejected in their own right. I have known people who never raised their heads from the burden of everyday, so-called 'simple' needs (as if survival were something simple), and others harrowed by less visible constraints than those which bear down on the poorest (the Arabs lying on the streets of Algiers, eyes covered in flies, the dispossessed), and like so many of the young men and women who search for meaning in our time, I walked among them, feeling that I too was deprived, like them in some way also pushed away from having a sense of meaning. I believe that human beings are equal, for what else can a life be compared to if not itself, its brief span? And I cannot tolerate the fact that we do not share the same rights to manage our fate and our intrinsic, unconstrained, liberatory diversity—simply because we are blocked by the needs imposed by power, by money, by everything that turns some into the objects of others' choices. This, for me, is 'politics', it is 'the others'—it is not a privation. It's like breathing. I would not live without air, and I suffocate in a world in which we're not free to communicate and realize ourselves due to all our differences of money and power. These are not the only matters that block the I; but they are the only intolerable ones, because they could be removed. And (without great success) I fight to remove them. Perhaps, within their texture, I could find a niche in which to live with myself and a few of those dear to me, but at the cost of depriving myself of all those others who I couldn't talk to and who could not communicate with me.

All the diversity of what is not in me enchants and determines me: I form myself, I am, in reacting to it. Is it a dream? I don't think so: it is the 'I'. And not a neutral 'I' in the sense invented for him 'but also for her'; it is the primary human condition, on which free and imposed differences grow and come to be established. Those who see things in this way will discover, as I did, that sexual difference is a plus that does eliminate the other claim; it articulates it. Those who view the world in this way are not martyrs: martyrs testify to something that others do not know. I am the daughter of a modernity that has testified to this on one side and another: there is no martyr here. I continue, at times with a kind of furious pleasure, to testify when some busybody says to me: 'But my dear, don't you see that today the drive is to be different? That your cleaning lady wants to be *different* from you? That there's no need to downplay the negritude at Pretoria, with its tragic aesthetic charge, and the old lords of Apartheid, for aren't they tragic too because—*et que vive la différence!*—sooner or later they'll end up slaughtered?'[6]

'But,' you'll say, 'Pretoria is far away and what can you do? Isn't it both torturous and presumptuous to wake up in the morning and think about writing an editorial, instead of living out your day better, in greater balance, opting for a more pragmatic set of experiences?' This is a sensible observation. I recognize that in this embracing of the whole world, this neurotic reading of the newspaper muttering: 'But this is intolerable', in this reaching for the pen or taking the floor, there is a certain Luciferian impulse. To want to live in the world, in the meeting/clashing with the other, in the mass of emotions, the expectations, the recognitions of a

---

6 Perhaps a reference to the Mamelodi Massacre of 1985, when the police opened fire on a demonstration of mainly women, just outside Pretoria, killing 13 people. [Trans.]

day's glance, of a common task, to live within relations of communication that—you're right—are a form of love, in all this there is a devilish need to say: 'The whole world is also something that belongs to me.' But you need to pick: either I am Lucifer, or I am a martyr. I fear that I am indeed Lucifer.

I fear this because I know the dangers, for both the self and the other, of the relation with the other for its own sake. Every I—or perhaps my own I, let's speak about what we have experience of—is both complex and weak for the drive to understand everything to be thrown off balance, to feel exposed by the collapse of the whole that escapes it and by a desire that finds no response to itself. This is not something known by women alone. Men have known it from the mists of time, crying out: 'Lord, why have you forsaken me? Why do you avert your gaze from me? I am losing myself in solitude.' It is David's lament, echoing in modern man: I am so delegitimated in my own eyes that I expect to draw from the love of another the certainty that I exist. The disquiet of an I not content with itself is as old as the world, but it is not the same thing as dependency: one is dependent if one attaches the beginning and end of oneself to another but not if one perceives the presence, otherness and indecision of a formed and finished being. Lucifer is infamous not only for his pride but also for his fall.

And I also know—I hope—the danger of turning to the rest of the world not only to say: 'Open up, speak, my hand is in yours' but to play a part in the old tale of: 'I will save you.' I will save him, her, society, nature, my cat. But isn't it the case that this stupid refrain risks deceiving more those who believe in the regenerative power of autonomy (in the sense that the more autonomous one is, the less one burns oneself up) rather than those who, instead of perceiving their autonomy as endangered by others, are instead constructed every day through a web of relations with that which I call the *other*—in order to underscore that which is outside of me, that which was born before and will come after me, that which does not share my structure and with which all I have in common, with any certainty, are the first and last questions? Indeed, whoever searches for a solution in the I—as a reply to the timeworn, slippery and reactionary warning not to pay attention to oneself—is led to believe, not so differently from those who warn of altruism, that others *must* conserve themselves in the same way. The others are always, I think, those to whom we are tempted to point out a path: 'I know what you need to do. Use yourself up more. Or conserve yourself more.' In more refined creatures it acts as a suggestion, elicits a real anxiety. In the political sphere it is the recurring temptation of whomever has power and the suggestion becomes something else. But to avoid this danger we must close our eyes and say: 'Let's not use ourselves up for this or that. Isn't it useless anyway?' Is it true, as I read in a recent issue of the journal *Alfabeta*, that we theorize a minimal ethics because the questions 'What must I do?' 'What should one do?' 'What will you do?' would be an intrusion into the precious and composite monads that we are, resolved not to speak, not to see, not to feel?

Thus, simply thinking about nothing less than the relation between person and history—for which I'm chastised—is a matter of modesty, not dependency. Because, as I have written in the past, I will never be truly 'explained' by history, nor can history be explained by summing up everything that has happened. Rather, this can only be done *through* history, not *looking beyond it*; by choosing where, how, when and within which limits to intervene. I am not singing the praises of some kind of devotion here but advancing a vision of the self and the world: this is not a sermon, it is an idea of what living means to me, and it is no more arrogant than retreating into the self.

Above all, this is not, in my eyes, a source of pain, the nail in the cross: that is far more deeply embedded in the turbulence of the I, something we carry with us as our key to interpret the other, rather than receiving it from them. We are finished, circumscribed, concluded in time just as much as in the extension of our minds: this is not 'dramatic' in the sense of suffering; it is 'tragic' in the sense of insoluble. And I do not know how to 'be a sex' if not through modes of this acknowledgment, this consciousness: within this lies everything that I know and have discovered about man and woman—which I might also call the neuter of the species, for it is from and through this common condition that the ancient act of the domination of one sex over another was waged, and upon which was then built a decalogue of differences, as old as the oldest books. It from this I want to free myself.

I am not sure that I will free myself through the praise of difference. Because there are two possibilities here. *Either* difference is the product of a state of subalternity, in which within the role assigned to woman her 'I' has acquired certain profound wisdoms, but only those (the territory of the heart) and every time that I draw on them I know that they are *mine* but also belong to a 'me' that has been trained for millennia to dig deep only within that patch of earth. *Or* the act of domination has cancelled out my initial substance, an essence experienced only by the very first woman, Lilith, and which every now and again comes forth in the desire for an image of a totally autonomous femininity—totally autonomous *because* totally different. Yet here we are no longer dealing with autonomy but with an impossibility of communication between two different orbits: two human species, two cultures, two languages—one which has always been speaking, the other mute. The idea of difference is either a 'differentiating method', that is, it examines a relationship *between two parts*, or it is a closed circle, an impasse.

It is not the case that those who think in this way only discover the person late in life; for my generation in particular, the person was the first centre because we are the children of Kafka, Melville and Dostoevsky. They discover that the person is in fact not 'private', that it is nothing other than acting upon everything that our historical destiny has in common, what we encounter on being born, which we will perhaps transform to some extent, and for the most part will be obliged to endure as we live. This complicates the idea of *acting among others*, with others, but it does not reduce its weight—in the end it renders every slogan inert. It forces us—in all the moments and modes of the present, the subjunctive, the conditional—to conjugate hope, hopes, blurring all the beaten tracks, rendering the 'I' and the other evermore problematic. It might make one smile when I say: 'And this too enchants me', since it is impossible to say as much without counting the bruises on one's body. It is dangerous enough simply to defend the private 'I' from the public one, as if they were two entirely divided fields with their different battles, both lost and won. When Lea wrote of a 'red asceticism',[7] she was quite right to laugh

---

7 Lea Melandri, *L'infamia originaria. Facciamola finita col cuore e la politica* (Milan: L'Erba Voglio, 1977), p. 39.

at this division, accompanied as it is, for the most part, by affidavits made by the monstrous law-making of the public 'I', monstrous both in the face of others and of the self. But when the 'I' defines itself in relation to the other, as a weave and texture that both is and is not the same thing (they become the same thing, I think, on the last day of one's life: because in that moment the design is fixed into the weave and cannot be changed any more, with all of its fraying and colours and errors), then one becomes very wary about values and laws. The conscience of the other is a risk, communication brings with it a sense of limitations. Above all else, ethics is an attention to rhythm, to the sound the other emits.

Is it not in this spirit that women have allowed me to listen to them, and have sometimes listened to me? I don't believe they think that having cried like an eagle (or a hen) with the pain of so many, and against them, has been the high road to my own negation. I do not believe it even when, contradictorily, they criticize my 'sacrifices' or when Lea, shaking her beautiful head of red hair, stares at me with amused, scared, wary eyes as if to say: 'But you're mad, mad—save yourself!' And her pen, in rewriting some of my words in order to hear them better, asks: 'But why so much pain? She could have had so much more peace.' Perhaps. I don't know, I've never tried. I do not know that 'autonomy' but I have conquered another in the time I've been given—though I admit only through an exhausting effort, with its deaths and casualties. I am not tempted by it: if I want to become better acquainted with myself, it is because I want to know more—about myself and the other . . . I would like to know everything, even the day of my death—perhaps I would then live in a more painful way, but maybe also a richer one. But let us leave behind such devilish whims and turn to being a woman. It is not only my personal paradox that we discover this late, through living life: all women have discovered it late, because being *a priori* a woman— something we got from the first 'Pretty little girl, who will you marry when you grow up? Daddy!' and so on with the years up until our first loves—it is eventually being a woman that we have put in question. We had to negate it in order to ask ourselves: 'But who am I, what does 'woman' mean?' This is what I meant when I wrote that feminism forced us into a revolutionization and, for those who want to revolutionize the world, thus necessitated a double revolutionization. It also wounded us, sundering us from some truths about ourselves, because we now had to verify that those truths had indeed been communicated, an activity that also freed us from a swathe of comfortable pleasures—aside from freeing us from a specific destructive oppression, one that for many women, far too many, remains to this day. (I am speaking of all those women who are of little interest to the woman who already feels free and confident; the outcasts, those who have not had the time nor the opportunity to understand, the manure on the new earth of the feminine). Being a woman is thus not an *a priori*, any more than being conscious of oneself as individual consciousness is, a self: nothing here is immediate, everything is the outcome of a journey. For many it came earlier, for me later. But I do not know to what extent for other women this 'arrival', this leap in time, *also* solidly turned into an 'in the beginning there was my being a woman.'

Let me explain. There is an *a priori* fact to sexuality, one strongly established by social history (the act of domination). The *a priori* fact is determined but not particularly meaningful, like having two legs and a limited lifespan; biology is determined but it only becomes important when it is perceived by consciousness as the grounds for or the impossibility of a range of options. This is the level on which the priority or otherwise of being a woman is posed for each of us today—not on any more elementary a basis. It is on this level that— 'confusedly', as Lea says[8]—I perceive and, to some extent, reframe the priority of being woman. Because my path cannot be changed; I have structured my person in a different way.

---

8 Melandri, *Una vita scritta.*

Lea says, therefore 'not as a *whole* person'.[9] And why not? If, as I have tried to explain, the choice of meeting/encounter/confrontation[10] with the other is not dependency, why should it not be 'whole'? What does it mean, anyway, to be a 'whole woman'? A 'whole person'? If it means self-determining—irrespective of the historical moment and the egos and the conditions surrounding her—I think this is an illusion, a belief in being alone in and for oneself. If this is the dream of a harmonious reflection of the universe within us, then it is precisely that: a dream. An experience that is not a dream is either dual or a fusion. And the wholeness of a determination—that is, neither more nor less than self-scrutiny, the attempt to understand oneself, and the attempt to scrutinize and understand the other—is tantamount to the effort to reduce to the bare minimum the inevitable fate that is the dissipation of the self, hidden suffering, the cry we carry within ourselves from childhood, the attempt to live out our own finitude with lucidity.

I am a woman who has passed through a good part of this century, seeing it and seeing myself within it. *First* woman and *then* an eye watching myself and the other? I don't know and it's not very important. Woman is a predetermination, like being born to an Austro-Italian mother and father, here rather than in

---

9 Melandri, *Una vita scritta*.
10 In the original: *confronto/incontro/scontro*. [Trans.]

Zambia, from one matrix and not another. The *a priori* givens are many: but my life is an adventure with this predetermination, a way of using it and freeing myself from it. Do we really want to call this 'neutral'? An unaware mimicry of the other's command? The fact of being a woman who is *powerful and unhappy*—a fairly ridiculous figure, no? And melancholy to boot. Because, of course, one assumes that the second adjective, 'unhappy', stems from the illusion of the first, 'powerful'. Win what, win what? Some women who struggle with power continue to echo the intolerable Gertrude Stein, the American in Paris, to the point of exasperation.[11] I know what I would like to win, but it has little to do with power. Concrete individuality—*my* concrete individuality —is the concreteness of the days I have passed, days that cannot be liquidated in a mad rush for martyrdom, an impossible sanctification. I'm joking of course.

---

11 A reference to Stein's libretto for Virgil Thomson's opera *The Mother of Us All*, and this exchange between Susan B. Anthony and her confidante, Anne:

> ANNE. But Susan B., you fight and you are not afraid. And you will win. Win what? Win the vote for women [. . .]. Yes, some day the women will vote, and by that time [. . .].
>
> SUSAN B. By that time it will do them no good. Because having the vote, they will become like men. They will be afraid. Having the vote will make them afraid. Oh, I know it. But I will fight for the right, for the right to vote for them, even though they become like men, become afraid like men.
>
> [Trans.]

A final comment: writing as the outlying trench in a battle already lost on the grounds of being and doing. How could it be otherwise? For me at least, writing is a way of speaking about what we have lived and attempted; and as much as my own writing might be mediocre, it represents a form given to this experience. Even political writing, even the writing of slogans which—thanks be to God and good sense, I have never cultivated—is an exploration of the aesthetic field, a pleasure that is not provided by being and doing. I make sure not to underestimate this: otherwise, I wouldn't write. But I also don't mistake this for being and doing *in toto*: we would have to view ourselves as prophets, as discoverers of ideas, as inventors of sublime harmonies for writing not to also be a substitute for life itself. Can I say—can I whisper—that the idea of the great writer, convinced of their greatness, has always seemed ridiculous to me? From Kafka onwards, how could writing—for our generation—appear as anything other than an extreme refuge, the testimony of a loss?

It will not be that—if I can close with a pinch of malice—for those women who will invent a feminine writing, feminine language, that is, *not* the language of man as we have known it till now and, alas, continue to employ. That will be the new civilization . . . perhaps it'll turn out that way. This new femininity of the future does not excite me much because—as a woman with a name and surname and a date of birth and a good number of years behind her—I'm still myself struggling *within* the mixed culture of domination. But it is *mixed* (and it is not because we have not written much that women are not particularly present within culture and literature; we are always the 'sex that is not a sex', as if it really 'were not'); half-baked, unsettled, contradictory, full of impoverished masculinities and great insights that someone might mistakenly label neutral, if 'neutral' meant anything. In my view it doesn't, but the non-sexed is not that third sex which I think Aristophanes speaks of in the *Symposium*.[12] Diotima speaks through the mouth of Socrates, who has listened to and learnt from her, the foreigner. Is Socrates' speech, his narration about her 'neuter'? There is a host of issues here, as one intuits from the strange title of this journal.[13] Concerns, intuitions, flashes, glimmers, journeys in the darkness, lights. Please, listen to mine with leniency.

---

12 'There were three kinds of human beings, that's my first point—not two as there are now, male and female. In addition to these, there was a third, a combination of those two; its name survives, though the kind itself has vanished. At that time, you see, the word 'androgynous' really meant something: a form made up of male and female elements, though now there's nothing but the word, and that's used as an insult.'—Plato, *Symposium*, 189e, in *Complete Works* (John M. Cooper ed.) (Indianapolis: Hackett, 1997), p. 473. [Trans.]

13 The subtitle of the journal in which this piece was first published, *Lapis* (Latin for stone, as in lapis lazuli) translates as 'Paths of feminine reflection'. [Trans.]

2

A HUSSAR CALLED HOPE *

In centuries past, what drove some women to disguise themselves as men? The need to free oneself from one's sex through an impossible mimesis of the male one is far too easy a reply. The question of sexual transvestism is extremely old and does not imply the refusal of an identity. Usually, it represents a kind of cunning: a man dresses as a woman or a woman as a man to reach a certain aim or cross an otherwise arduous passage. It is a temporary experience which ends with an unveiling and everyone's re-entry into their own gender.

The asymmetry of the sexes means that a man takes on a woman's disguise when, for example, he returns to his usurped realm, while a woman usually feigns being a man in order to avoid amorous propositions or violations, of the kind a young woman without

---

* First published in *Lapis. Percorsi della riflessione femminilc*, 3 March 1989.

home or homeland could be exposed to while set on different ends. They are always precarious beings, wandering unknown territories or returning to lands where they are not yet or no longer welcome. They are always young, in keeping with the similarly smooth faces and slim bodies of the ephebe and the maiden. And usually, transvestitism is a kind of a game, though not without ambiguity, as if in seemingly changing sex one also revealed an unconscious bisexuality. Shakespeare more than touches upon this truth: in *As You Like It*, Rosalinda tries to seduce the man she loves dressed as a man, while in *Twelfth Night*, Viola as a man is the object of the unlucky Olivia's affections, but then becomes the object of Duke Orsino's once she plays a man transforming into a woman. Yet it is not always a game: Joan of Arc, condemned for wearing masculine clothing, did so simply to fulfil her vocation as warrior ('If not me, who? If not now, when?'). While female warriors of legend may dress themselves as men, they are not crossdressing—consider Bradamante and Clorinda, the first 'emancipated' women.[1] It is emancipation to assume male clothing and masculine roles *as women*, shedding the hindrance of female habits, and with a lesser transgression than one might think at first, since this is a

---

1 Bradamante is a knight heroine in Matteo Maria Boiardo's *Orlando Innamorato* (1483–1495) and Ludovico Ariosto's *Orlando Furioso* (1516); Clorinda is a warrior woman in Torquato Tasso's poem *Jerusalem Delivered* (1581). [Trans.]

kind of homage to masculinity as the highest mode of being, entered into by so few that it does not represent a real disturbance to the social and familial order.

Tranvestisism at the dawn of modernity takes on yet more forms. Sexual ambiguity is not hidden in the memoirs of Chevalier d'Éon,[2] nor does the travelling in men's clothing of Kleist's overly loved sister seem merely functional.[3] This returns us to many of the major questions around the issue of sex posed in that moment of German culture, equally present in her brother's works. When the emancipation of women expanded in the twentieth century, it made no sense for a woman to dress as a man any more. That history is finished. Today the transvestite, whether female or (more often) male, simply represents a relation to sex different from the physiological one.

In Nadezhda A. Durova's *The Cavalry Maiden*, we are presented with a very different phenomenon, that of a woman who dresses as a man due to her despair

---

2 *La Vie Militaire, politique, et privée de Mademoiselle d'Éon* (1779) is the title of the ghost-written memoirs of the French spy, diplomat and soldier Charles-Geneviève-Louis-Auguste-André-Timothée d'Éon de Beaumont (1728–1810), who lived their first forty-nine years as a man (while also presenting as a woman for the purposes of subterfuge) and their last thirty-three as a woman. Bram Stoker devoted a chapter of *Famous Impostors* (1910) to the Chevalier d'Éon. [Trans.]

3 Ulrike von Kleist (1774–1849), Heinrich von Kleist's half-sister. [Trans.]

at not being able to be a woman.[4] Nadezhda Durova was a real person. Born in 1783, she was married at eighteen and had a son. At the age of 21 she fled from her husband and returned to her family, from whom she later ran away on the night of her Saint's Day, cutting off her hair and donning a hussar's uniform, leaving her own clothes on the riverbank (to her neighbours' benefit) but taking her favourite horse with her, Alkid (a clear sign to her father that she had not drowned). Accepted by the nearest regiment as a young man, she served in the campaign against Napoleon up to the battle of Borodino, first as a private and then as an officer; she was decorated with a medal of honour and went on leave in 1816. At this point she was thirty-three, having spent ten years in the army as a man. When something later betrayed her and she was revealed as a soldier-woman by Tsar Alexander I, Nadezhda nevertheless continued to behave as a soldier, including in matters of protocol, embarrassing the Tsar, who didn't know how to react; she persuaded him that being forbidden from serving as an officer would have thrown her into despair. Alexander thus kept the secret of her sex and—although Nadezhda does not

---

4 Nadezhda A. Durova, *The Cavalry Maiden: Journals of a Russian Officer in the Napoleonic Wars* (Mary Fleming Zirin trans.) (Bloomington: Indiana University Press, 1988). Rossanda refers to the recently published Italian translation: *Memorie del cavalier-pulzella* (Pia Pera ed. and trans.) (Palermo: Sellerio, 1988). The original *Zapiski kavalyerist devitsy* was published in 1836. [Trans.]

admit this explicitly—had her discretely protected by the highest levels of command, from Buxtehowen to Suvorov. Only once the Russian campaign was over and the French defeated did Nadezhda return as a woman within society, received at first with great applause and curiosity, then with coldness from men and women alike, as someone who did not belong to one sex or the other. She thus lived out the next fifty years alone in a village, writing; she dressed as a woman but took long excursions in the forest, by foot or on horse, something unusual for a woman; and in the village, where the children brought her stray cats and dogs because she loved people and nature, respect and affection meant she was called by a male name and patronymic. She was buried with military honours in 1866. These are the facts, which take a peculiar form in her memoirs, written around 1835 and so highly appreciated by Pushkin that for some time it was believed that they were a work of his own (a confusion that was not repeated after the subsequent publication of her novels and short stories). There are many redactions in her memoirs. First of all, the title, in which the word for 'cavalier' [де́вица] sounds like the word for 'maiden' or 'virgin' [дева]. And in fact, the tale radically excises the experience of marriage and motherhood, imperceivable in the brief lines describing her unhappiness on her sixteenth birthday, when Nadezhda began to plan her escape to the army. A dextrous narrative move (or one of memory itself?)

makes it seem as though presenting oneself to the regiment, after having run away from home, as a seventeen-year-old raring to fight against the family's wishes, was a common enough occurrence in the period.

But she was twenty-three, and her contemporaries who read the memoir would not have overlooked this fact. Not only did this rejuvenation make presenting herself as a man more plausible—a seventeen-year-old male is usually beardless—but it also seemed to facilitate her abiding as a man. We are also given to understand that the commanders maintained a protective watch over these soldiers, little more than boys, feeling a kind of responsibility towards them and entrusting them to an older mentor who took care of them—aside from during the fighting itself when they were asked the same as any other officer. Nadezhda's noble birth is essential here, because it separates her from the soldier's life, along with its language and customs. As for the officers themselves, either the young woman was extremely able or their manners were immaculate—or perhaps memory has again energetically redacted some detail. As it stands, not only do we read about the nights passed together on the bivouac or the death-filled slumber lying next to one another on the field in the wake of battle but also of the long periods in the barracks, when Nadezhda shared a room with one officer or another, or more than one, but—so it seems—no one suspected her sex nor made homosexual advances.

'Finally, I have a room to myself' is the only annotation: these were not the times to speak about the body, and certainly not of menstruation. Without doubt the young maiden-cavalier occasionally had to find her daily privacy and yet apparently no one discovered her. If she received an ugly wound in battle, or caught a fever, she kept it to herself because, as she writes: 'A good officer does not complain.' But how could she have been seen by a doctor? Either way, her memoirs claim it was possible for a woman to appear as a young man among men. The book does not say how matters stood ten years' later, when Lieutenant Durov was meant to be 27. And in truth, the book does not tell us that by then it was known 'Durov' was actually 'Durova', but the emperor's protection and her regular behaviour as an officer guaranteed a mutual silence.

What is not said in the memoirs is much less important, however, than what is said, and how. In the Italian edition, at least, we lack the central part, the meeting with the Tsar, and therefore the discovery of her sex (perhaps through a letter that she wrote to her father, which fell into the hands of a general); we do read about her life from childhood through to her time in the army and then the trials of war. The narrative begins with her mother's flight from the family home to marry a captain, by whom she had at least three children. From the beginning, her mother awaited a son in trepidation and had already given him a name—

but instead a girl came into the world, one who was unusually large and ugly. It was her, Nadezhda, whose name means 'hope'. But she was a great disappointment, one from which her mother never recovered. She nursed her reluctantly, while the girl hurt her breast and struggled so much that one day her mother, out of her mind, threw her out of the window of the carriage, screaming. Her father, riding next to them, turned white in the face and clasped her to him, certain he was holding a small corpse between his arms.

Who told Nadezhda of this violent refusal, this near assassination? And when? Having miraculously survived, the mother still found her child so intolerable that she entrusted her to an elderly guardian, who took care of her and taught her how to ride a horse, an activity which her mother made her renounce when she was older, forcing her instead to turn to lacework; she was forbidden from running around or going outside. She was asked to resign herself to who she was: irremediably ugly and wretched, as she was told by her mother. For a few years, she eagerly sent her away to stay with her grandmother or an aunt, who let her run free in her beloved forests, taught her good manners, how to brush her hair, how to dress; they treated her like a young girl gifted with grace. Nadezhda writes that, had she been allowed to remain there, she would have accepted her fate as a woman within the warmth of an affectionate and loving family. She even falls in love . . .

though at a distance. But she must return to the rigours of the north and her mother, who only loves her (beautiful) second daughter and Vasily, the son for whom she had always hoped. Everyone had been born right, except her. So she decides to leave, and the first chapter ends with the alternating feelings of the night of her flight and her arrival at the hussar regiment at dawn. Here her adventures as a soldier ought to begin, but instead the second chapter goes back and, without respect for chronological order, retells the story of her childhood and her relationship with her mother. She writes not only that her mother did not love her but that she imbued her with the feeling she could not be loved. Introjecting this claim, the young Nadezhda engaged in the most reckless mischief and met with ever-increasing reproach. This maternal enmity not only convinced her she was unlovable but also impeded her from finding affection elsewhere: a beloved puppy was taken from her and, even more swiftly, a grouse of which she had grown very fond, lacking anything better. A sobbing Nadezhda takes its cold feathered body to bed with her; she is discovered, and the poor grouse thrown out of the window (like her?). As if this were not enough, her mother imparts on her all the unhappiness of being a woman, describing the female fate in dark detail and stubbornly forcing her into it. Wasn't it she herself who was first damned by her father and then betrayed by a redundant husband? But her mother could not remove herself from the situation, and so Nadezhda must pass hours closed in her room, working away at the damned lace.

It is her mother's destructive unhappiness that leads Nadezhda not so much to an eccentric choice but, paradoxically, to obey the image of herself that her mother inculcates. She ought to have been born a man to be accepted. So she will live as one. No one can love her, so marriage and motherhood would be a mistake, to be struck from her mind. Disguised as a man she will escape her destiny, living without being rejected at every moment. And she can stay by the side of 'the only being that has ever truly loved me', her wondrous steed Alkid, who can be ridden by her alone and who carries her like an arrow, following her around and affectionately chewing at her hair and shoulders. When Alkid dies—through her own carelessness or negligence—it will be the only real bereavement she suffers, an insurmountable, endless grief. Besides this, only solitude. Nadezhda does not pretend for a moment to be a man, describing the war with a sense of duty, the only 'sense' that she is allowed—and pity. Twice she arrives too late, or not at all, to rescue two casualties, receiving severe reprimands. She knows how to describe with communicative strength what it means to lay still under the bullets and cannon fire when one has to 'cover' a manoeuvre: the soldiers pointlessly debate it, hoping to evade their inescapable fate, while a nobleman knows how to look death in the face in order to respect his country and himself. But when she writes of hand-to-hand combat she does not tell us who or how many she killed, simply of her numb and painful hands having to raise the unsheathed sabre under the sharp north wind. And after the fighting she sees the horror of her horse riding through the dead, and describes the desolate fields of bodies, lying down, naked because everyone is poor. She is also poor and needs an overcoat but cannot face removing one from a corpse. The war is cold, tiredness, hunger, blood, and must be faced with fortitude, but without declarations other than the formal (perhaps comforting) homage to the fatherland, and an intelligent interest in strategy. The only joy is to be found in waking up in the hazy mornings, the tents filled with campfires, music and something warm to fill your stomach.

In moments of relaxation, she had to remove herself from the eyes of women, because they could not be deceived. Either through malice or mischief, they would whisper to her: 'You're a woman, you're not fooling me.' Nadezhda does not wait for anyone to denounce her: she is afraid and flees. If her sex had been revealed, she would have been sent home in a sea of gossip, casting a shadow over her and her acts of valiance. For a woman, there is no way out.

The Italian edition skips the part relating how she came to know of the early death of her mother. But a summary tells us that she died finally knowing, on her deathbed, what Nadezhda had written to her father, and which he had then shown to his unloved partner: 'So she blames me for everything,' the unfortunate woman said, turning her face to the wall. These were her last words. Nadezhda remained certain that she had tormented her mother from the moment she came into the world right up to her last dying breath.

That's how she lived. Neither as a woman nor as a man, excluding herself from all affection for not having merited the very first kind, due to the 'mistake' of her birth. A leap into the relative abstractness of relations among men—and then into writing—perhaps saved her from madness, but at a great cost.

If we were to ask Nadezhda why she cross-dressed, she would respond neither like the Shakespearean heroine nor like the more modern emancipated woman: she lacks the extrinsic goal, that is, appearing as a man in order to realize an external aim. She acts like a man because a woman can then live differently from how she has been both moulded and devalued. Her transvestism has no end that cannot be identified with the means. Later she would explain—from the viewpoint of one who already knows the path that could not be taken—how the disguise could only have lasted for a brief period, the one permitted by the contours of the body. After this, it became necessary for her to obtain a different status than that assigned to a woman in the Russia of the time. The book emphasizes how this different status does not just imply the power to have other ambitions—even if some later writings would speak of the 'responsible' role that women can and must now exercise in the ambit of their civil and social relations. Rather, it means living free from one's body and freely choosing a discipline that is not imposed by the patriarchy. Even military discipline is preferable, because much is asked and expected of the 'noble', and to a great extent the discipline is open to a wide range of self-realizations.

These realizations are precluded to her, as the transvestite that she is—what she experienced instead was throwing herself into battle in front of her troops, as a model of bravery and tragedy, a pedagogic figure of self-overcoming. In other words, she experienced a system of relations that was not entirely other-directed—especially in her own case, since her life is based on a free choice.[5] But her memoirs also describe an exit from the social status of women in order to experiment with the freedom of the body as a bridge to a vast world. Nadezhda discovered the woods late in life, or the thrill of riding an attentive, nervous creature, things she was not allowed as a child and could not live

---

5 By 'other-directed', Rossanda refers implicitly to David Riesman (with Nathan Glazer and Reuel Denney), *The Lonely Crowd: A Study of the Changing American Character* (New Haven, CT: Yale University Press, 1950). [Trans.]

without from that moment on. The limits imposed on the body of a young girl by the rules of proper behaviour hit her like a shocking mutilation, an intolerable physical imprisonment, a cheap, forced repetition. Being able to pass day and night in the woods or the fields or running or riding a horse until you fall asleep is so essential as to be prioritized over sexual relations. Here a free woman is not so free as to be able to imagine and desire a free sexuality: the image handed down to us of motherhood's unhappy sexuality remains definitive. It is also significant how the importance given to the maternal figure precludes any consideration of her own maternity. Pia Pera, the editor and translator, observes that Nadezhda excises three of the four years in which she was both wife and mother from her story 'with a scalpel blade', freeing up the integral form of the narrative. But we might cast some doubt on this. Nadezhda is no Amazon: she does not renounce her sex and speaks with tenderness of her first potential love. Her silence cannot be easily explained. There might have been a traumatic memory of sexual experience. Perhaps she denied the trauma. Perhaps she felt guilty about her husband or children. Though she wrote to her father, she nevertheless does not seem to have ever written to her husband, whom she had left two years before. And the lie of her virginity? An internal erasure, an ode to the rules of romance or an homage to social rules? A fear of presenting herself not only through a unique adventure but also as a woman who abandoned a child? There is only one unmistakable message that this text imparts to us: that the female sex is unhappy, denied by and to itself, but that one can—one must—live it differently.

3

THÉROIGNE DE MÉRICOURT : NEITHER COMMONER NOR LADY *

'She was a soldier' writes Annarita Buttafuoco in a valuable essay on the women of the French Revolution.[1] But was she really? The image, or fantasy, of the beautiful warrioress runs across the historical literature, whether right-wing or radical, up to the present day.

Such figures have appeared ever since Michelet, alongside more famous women like Marie Antoinette, Olympe de Gouges and Manon Roland (all of whom Michelet loved because he was infatuated with his young wife). Sometimes they emerge from the ranks of the nobility educated by Enlightenment thinkers and protected by their ancestry (even when they are

---

* First published in *Lapis. Percorsi della riflessione femminile*, 4 June 1989.

1 Annarita Buttafuoco, 'Libertà, ugualianza, fraternità: per chi?' in *Atti del seminario Esperienza storica femminile nell'età moderna e contemporanea* (Rome: La Goccia, 1988).

libertines). Or they may rise up from the crowd of common women who, for the first time, descend from the
banlieues into the sites of history, invading them and
sometimes putting their decisive stamp on events
through a protagonism and violence that put an end to
any hesitation. They are the *sans culottes* of the short
skirt, the ribbed corset, the neckerchief thrown around
generously uncovered shoulders, and a bonnet or red
liberty cap with a cockade on their heads. What they
share is that this moment would be stained with their
blood. The heads of Marie Antoinette, Olympe de
Gouges and Manon Roland would fall, as would that
of Charlotte Corday, Marat's silent assassin, or the
women among the *Enragés*, Pauline Léon and Claire
Lacombe. Aside from this, they held little in common.
Between the demands levelled by the women of the
nobility and those arising from among female shop-
keepers and commoners there is only a shared desire
to be differentiated, but with a wavering sense of their
rights as a sex (*du sexe* as they said of themselves); that
is, a sense of those rights about which the best speech
was not provided by themselves—not even by the
impassioned Olympe—but by Nicolas de Condorcet.
Violence, blood and havoc would be employed to
silence these women, along with the few who defended
them in the Assembly.

It is far from easy to extricate the individual figures
from the dense and murky imaginary transmitted by

history. There falls upon them both a kind of shadow and a phantasmatic projection. This is how Théroigne de Méricourt comes to be seen as a 'soldier'—indeed, a leader of soldiers, the wielder of a ferocious blade— a figure who stands as a symbol for all women, a demonstration of the fact that history is unable to contain the female world without mystifying it. She is truly invisible. Not even sympathetic histories, not even those from a feminine standpoint that have recently emerged from the academy, have managed truly to see her.

We owe the reconstruction of who she really was to the recent work of Élisabeth Roudinesco—supported by views 'from the women's side' provided by Élisabeth Badinter—in *Théroigne de Méricourt. Une femme mélancolique sous la Révolution*.[2] Here we read of a slim and restless woman, brought to Paris after having lost her mother, taught to sing by a society lady and to read and write by an English officer, a man who later abandoned her to a lavish life and a solid income. She moved between Paris, London and Rome, right up to the eve of the Revolution, associating with people of dubious character whom she did not love but with or

---

2 Élisabeth Roudinesco, *Théroigne de Méricourt. Une femme mélancolique sous la Révolution* (Paris: Éditions du Seuil, 1989). [In English translation: *Madness and Revolution: The Lives and Legends of Théroigne de Méricourt* (Martin Thom trans.) (London: Verso, 1991).—Trans.]

from whom she defended her assets. She became ill—perhaps from syphilis—and lost her young daughter. She is a marginal figure, neither commoner nor, like Olympe de Gouges, a lady. Manon Roland was firmly established within a family and a party, while Léon and Lacombe were clearly women of the people, connected to a political group as well as a profession.

Théroigne's social, intellectual and emotional oscillation was channelled spontaneously into the days of May 1789, when France leaves its stagnation behind. She was around 30, alone, and every morning she followed the decrees of the Estates General and annotated them; she knew the members of the Tribunal, hosting them at her house, she founded one or two clubs and partook in the debates of the day. She did not love, but reacted emotionally only on impulse, running freely between ideas. She wanted to be among those who acted on those ideas. She wanted to be 'other' and represented this by always dressing as an 'Amazon', in a woman's horse-riding outfit. She had three pairs of Moroccan trousers (white, black and red), an overskirt, a large, feathered hat perched on a powdered head and silk sashes. When she joined the crowds—to which she does not belong—she carried a sword and two pistols that she never used; but she eagerly took the floor, for instance speaking at the Assembly with the legislators' kind permission. She left her mark on historical memory as a blood-thirsty warrioress by her elegant, eccentric dress, her fervent words, and her presence during a fight in which, among others, a grossly misogynist journalist called Suleau was killed. She is also remembered for her appeal—in one of her few surviving speeches—for the formation of a women's battalion for the defence of the country (she was not the only woman to propose this).

In truth she was a small, single, ill, restless woman who discovered a passion for politics and searched for her part and identity within it, despite insufficient training and a situation that exposed her to misogyny's most violent attacks, from both the right and the left. Perhaps she was second only to Marie Antoinette in eliciting the spirits of masculine hatred, as evidenced by her depictions as Maenad, madwoman, femme fatale, conspirator, her entire body invoked as an oozing sore; it is worthwhile studying this misogynist reaction and its phantasms. She never replies. This is simply a war of words, and she knows it well. She prefers the company of educated friends and, even if with some condescension, she admires them; she spends her time around the Jacobin clubs without, however, being part of them. She did not know the other women of the Revolution, and unlike Olympe de Gouges, was not guillotined; at the peak of danger she fled to Belgium, later returning. One day in 1793, while at the Convention, like every morning, a group of common women attacked, stripped and whipped her to humiliate the woman who they deem a Girondin. Like Olympe, Théroigne felt uneasy taking a clear political position but she prioritized her sex even less than her. It was Marat who saved her from the furious attacks and the satisfied stares of the gossipmongers; Marat, with his fiery tones and his body pocked by a horrible disease, was loved by the women of the Revolution—women about whom he never wrote—perhaps due to some strange identification with a voiceless sex trapped within a martyred body.

From this point onwards, Théroigne's wits started to leave her. Her mind already flickered with strange images that interrupted the otherwise entirely polite reasoning of her notes ('A house with a bronze elevation and a cellar carpeted in black, where a woman stands on the body of the enemy, a man, who would have been defeated had I not landed a punch'). She escaped the Terror because she had been checked into the Hôtel-Dieu, the hospital where women without families ended up, sick in their bodies and sick of themselves. From here she went to the Salpêtrière, overcome by a depressive psychosis—Pinel's famous *mania*—and for twenty years she became the object of Esquirol's nascent psychiatric observations. The abyss between imagination and reality was immense. It began with her name: Anne-Josephe Terwagne or Théroigne, born to a family of farmers in Marcourt, not far from Lièges. It was the royalist press that derisively called her not only Théroigne (they who called all her revolutionary friends by their surnames: Barnave, Sieyès and her greatest friend, Romme, the author of the new calendar) but also 'de Méricourt' to ridicule her for the backwater where she was born. She always signed with her real name but history recorded her with the other one. And with what face? There are many portraits of her, whether solo or in large scenes in which, moreover, she could not have participated: a thin Amazon with a slim face and burning eyes. The only image not submerged in fantasy is the portrait made by George F. M. Gabriel when she was recovering in hospital, which shows a pleasant complexion: not young by any means, harsh, staring ahead. The image is accompanied by a description of her clinical case, in which nothing about her is recognizable, save perhaps the repetition of obsessive acts, lying naked and expressionless in the hay or on the icy floor. She died in 1817 and was the subject of a didactic autopsy. Casts of her skull were made, models perplexing and painful in the stupefied bewilderment of death and wax. It is worth reflecting on the impossibility of recording the reality of the women who emerged in those years, and the concurrent creation of deformed figures, whether through adoration or enmity. This impossibility resounds with the fear of the irruption of a sex that is not only moved, as one says, by basic needs—such as the bread that Paris so cruelly lacked—but, when this is the case, goes out and does politics, becoming a new protagonist. The 'people', widely discussed for the first time, had become two-sexed, and women appeared to be the more bodily of bodies, filled with emotions, courage and cruelty; they are ever-present in front of the guillotine—which operates daily, carriages arriving ritualistically with noblemen and noblewomen in bonnets and shirts—perhaps as a revenge of sorts for centuries of humiliation and horror.

Those women who are not only bodies, cries and activity remain similarly blurry in historical memory, partly because their ideas cannot be classified like those of men. The general claim to personhood leads them to see that, among persons, women remained 'outside', unjustly oppressed—yet this recognition failed to develop either into a strong idea of the general overturning and revision of the relations of citizen, state, individual, power, division of powers, on which modern society will come to be structured, or into a real stance amid absolutely divisive choices in the battle of lives and ideas. Olympe de Gouges wavered between the republic and monarchy, supposedly due to the received idea of that 'equity' proper to the female sex, more generous and prepared to mediate. In truth, she failed to understand what was at stake. Théroigne wrote to Saint-Just shortly before his arrest, asking for help and giving advice, but ignoring the fact that he and Robespierre had already fallen. It does not seem possible that either she or de Gouges put the redemption of women before political allegiances, as some have claimed. It seems more likely that they simply didn't understand politics very well, having an enthusiastic but uneducated perception of events. Otherwise, one cannot explain why Olympe de Gouges (who chose and crafted her own name, partly Arcadian, partly noble—her real name was Marie Gouzes) addressed *Declarations of the Rights of Women* to Marie Antoinette, without doubt the woman least disposed to listen to her, given that anything that approached the *Declaration of Rights* of 1789—the text on which Olympe had freely modelled her own—filled her with horror.

Even though a queen, as a woman Marie Antoinette had known untold misery, beginning with the seven years of her husband's impotence in which she was submitted to all sorts of experiments so that the royal coitus could reach completion. And then there were the accusations that followed her everywhere. But she shut herself up in the icy protection of her palace, in her hatred for the Revolution and distaste for the common people, in her daily plotting with her mother, the terrifying Maria Theresa, and her brother Joseph. She lived and died as a bad queen. Conversely, nothing is certain about the revolutionary women if it is not that—as women, as a sex, as individuals—they were different from what their mothers had been and that their sisters were, and perhaps—as far as those who had a name and a role are concerned—they were also different from all those women who took to the streets with great uproar but without speaking, driven by the extremeness of the situation. In the end, it's as if there were two different mental processes taking place that could not overlap: on the one hand, a reflection on their own sex, forever excluded from politics; on the other, a reflection on the opening up of political society (one that *still* excluded them) in the context of an unprecedented situation in which new relations, as well as new forms of power and dependence were being forged. The historically immediate—the concrete formation of the Revolution through the transformation of choices and values— was so alien and unusual for them that they could not truly embrace it, could not truly intervene, truly choose. There is only one claim they could make: their right to also be full and equal citizens, because just like Condorcet they struggled against the still reigning distinctions (woman as inferior, with a lesser capacity for development, a slave to emotions and senses). But a long road still remained ahead of them due to their unfamiliarity with thinking through relations within the *polis*. This is the reason why they lived through the cascade of ideas and events of the Revolution without managing to leave any mark on it besides the sign of a now-recognized injustice. Due to a patent fear, their contemporaries could not forgive them, instead chasing them back into privacy or denouncing them; and thus they have come down to us as legendary relics, whether of valour or horror.

And just as some lost their heads, Théroigne herself went mad. Perhaps she would have gone mad all the same; perhaps in a certain sense she was always faced with the impossibility of everyday life, while during the upheaval between 1789 and 1795 her own troubles simply found a framework and a kind of calm. Certainly, the end of that revolutionary framework and the collapse of a self-image she had conquered with such effort—one that brought upon her the hatred of other women who publicly reduced her to the state of a naked and whipped female—pushed her into the long monologue of madness: the other half of her life.

4

DEPTH AND HISTORY *

While reading Giovanna Grignaffini's essay in *Lapis* on Claude Chabrol's *Story of Women* (1988), I was taken aback and said to myself: 'Ah, here's where my view differs from that of "women"—real women.'[1] Having watched *Story*, Grignaffini—partly due to her own particular experience of the images—proposed an interpretation of the role of Isabelle Huppert's hands in the film: exiled, impoverished hands, hands that work and perform abortions and take money and lie by her sides when she's taken to the guillotine. A woman's hands. I did not see them; I do not recall them. I was struck instead by a film that portrayed a woman who, *as a woman*, passes through the war as if it weren't happening, because it

---

* Published in *Lapis. Percorsi della riflessione femminile*, 7 March 1990.

1 Giovanna Grignaffini, 'Le mani della Storia', *Lapis. Percorsi della riflessione femminile*, 3 March 1989. [The reference is to *Une affaire de femme*, Chabrol's film about the life and death of Marie-Louise Giraud.—Trans.]

doesn't concern her; her concern is to deal with everyday chores and domestic misery in solitude, to free herself from an incapable husband whom she doesn't love,
eventually to be seduced (without passion) by an ugly
but capable collaborator (or a German, I don't recall)
and perform abortions for other women without sen-
timentality but not without pity, putting her 'knowledge' to work. Pétain's ferocious France remains in the
background, though in the end it sends her to her death
in the name of morality, to cover up its own cowardice.
All in all, I was fascinated by the estrangement that
allowed the protagonist apparently to become her own
master, while in truth making her blind to the forces
that crush her. In the end, she's so alone that she swears
at the Virgin Mary—that is, at bigoted and moralistic
mendacity, as though otherwise she would remain
unable to see her real enemies. This is a female destiny
that seems extraordinarily clear to me, written into history itself: that is, the specific and recurring story of
woman as scapegoat and detritus, a negative social symbol. This attribution and the multiplicity of meanings
that derive from it were to my mind the key to the film,
translated into the Huppert's acerbic body and hard
face. But her hands had escaped me. It seems however
that everything else escaped Giovanna Grignaffini, not
because she didn't see it but because it was irrelevant,
of secondary importance when compared to the totalizing language of the hands.

How could I not ask myself whether this viewpoint contained a different conception of the time and concrete space in which women exist, one so different as to interfere with the very possibility of communication? I had already considered the matter of 'women's temporality' with some discomfort when it was proposed to me not as an 'obligatory journey' but a 'positively different' experience. Furthermore, Lea's columns have often encouraged me to flatten out days, locations and their happenings, to reduce them to a low and fleeting hum, a distraction from the long time-periods and firmer ground of self-knowledge—knowledge like an excavation that constantly expands across the same ground, with the same tools, experimenting with how the most useful among these can be continually refined and examined (in the wake of Mantegazza,[2] Aleramo[3] and, in the background, Freud), in the same way that an archaeologist explores an area containing treasures and artefacts, making headway by keeping an eye carefully fixed on the precision and development of one's gestures, while constantly interrogating what the excavation might bring to light. Sometimes I think that, if I had to depict myself and Lea, I would paint her intent

2 Paolo Mantegazza (1831–1910), novelist, neurologist, physiologist and anthropologist who advocated the experimental use of cocaine. [Trans.]

3 Sibilla Aleramo (1876–1960), Italian feminist writer and poet. [Trans.]

on lifting up with her hands the find that refracts consciousness of the world and of the self, while I would draw myself all out of focus running without a pause towards some moving horizon, looking behind me and swerving as I press ahead, questioning unstable worlds—those of life and death—in all their diversity, while time passes, or rather flies by.

Is 'she' a woman, that running self? Many women have kindly told me no, because I run in the time and space of men, without interrogating myself about how essential it would be—after a long hibernation, partly fatal, partly creative—to rediscover being woman, female consciousness, identity, independence. Lea reminds me that this search is a political act, and she's right. She also reminds me that if one does this, then one cannot do other things (other than, according to Lea, existing and physically being). That is because research of this kind requires the engagement of all one's intellectual energies and necessitates a difficult distinction between that which is truly female and that which has been merely claimed as such—in the sense of being imposed from without.

But I question whether there really is a male and/or female essence, anchored to something other than the body and our historical mode of perceiving that corporeality. Other women tell me that other coordinates (the world, history), if they exist at all, do not entail women's research, because it is not women who have produced these; indeed, it is women's silence, their distance, that marks out the difference. Women who are conscious of themselves are extraneous to a world they have not made and thus have other issues— perhaps another world. These other issues can even interfere in one's *Bildungsroman*, to cite the title of a wonderful essay by Lidia Campagnano on 1969.[4] She holds together the world and her own self, but only by bringing the world back to the self and those serious choices that mark the self above all.

Some months back I wanted to try and reflect on these two or three levels of experience, these times and spaces, these dimensions of being female. Like Lea, I see this as a variation on a relation of the 'I' to the world that is not only a female relation. I wanted to try and show that the search into oneself must move across two levels—depth and history—because archetypes and symbols are also formed across these two levels, against which identity continually clashes, while also nurturing itself through its challenge to the world. But let's be frank.

I think that without moving across these two levels, any research will reproduce the illusion that we are 'outside of history', while in reality no one is truly outside

---

4 Lidia Campagnano, 'Una stagione densa come un romanzo di formazione', *il Bimestrale*, supplement to *il manifesto*, 12 December 1989. [Trans.]

it, even though many people, and nearly all women, have been set outside the 'decisive sites of history'.

Something else is at stake. And it seems meaningless to claim the narrow horizon that has been imposed on us as some kind of conquest. I have always seen it as a limitation, even though the women closest to me have never agreed with me. I have always thought that what we understand about ourselves should be the crystal that refracts the vision of the world of those who, having been 'set outside' and 'subjected to historical time', approach the world through the experience and distance of the excluded, that is, through the perspective that comes with knowing that the other exists in another and precluded dimension, and who thus have to gauge the other and their orbit with wisdom and a sense of relativity. The absence of decision is not a vote, nor is it even really an abstention from decision: it is the perception of the other side of decision, its density for those who cannot choose; it is simultaneously both relativity and coercion. Female autonomy has thus always appeared to me not as a retreat into the self but as an intervention into what is actually taking place— from a standpoint that, while different, is unwavering and can no longer be reduced to silence. But we were so distant from one another in this regard, among women, that a journal like *Orsa Minore,* for example, collapsed without my even understanding why. It was not so much the distance between myself and the others in terms of how we should also look beyond ourselves. The very act of looking beyond ourselves seemed to be either remote or irrelevant or a deviation—at the very best it appeared as something that only I was allowed because of my own biography. The biography of a woman who 'did politics,' and not just women's politics, or more precisely, who did politics among women and then, aside from this, also intervened in the 'other politics' or in the time of that 'other', leaping across a gap. I would have liked to dig further into this, to locate the innervation, the welded seam. Immediately. Because if not now, when? Tomorrow will be no easier than today: why should it be? What else would still need to develop so that woman's voice is heard not only with regard to her condition as a woman but as an 'individual' or a group of individuals who measure themselves against the search for their own history and identity? Such individuals do not propose this project simply as one of 'two' parties: the one who would keep watch over herself, looking for a way to find and free herself from something that is blocking and enveloping her, while nevertheless letting history and all its vicissitudes unfold 'outside'.

I write this in the last days of 1989, and the conditions are ripe for this kind of reflection. I am far from the din of my daily habits, in that strange kind of

Carloforte[5] a big metropolis can become if you do not usually live or work there, or know it well; you feel alone, as if standing before the sea. Paris in the great greys of winter is like a sea. I have no memories associated with the streets and for the most part the faces do not have names.

There is nothing outside that assails me or stops me from writing something to reassure myself, something that might bring me together with other women—not as someone who is simply a woman by biological accident, or because of what she does or is impelled to do, but instead by way of some kind of accent that she brings to bear on what she does and is impelled to do. But I do not know how to put this reflection into words, today, 28 December 1989. Everything that has happened this year stands between these thoughts and myself, the great disaggregation of the communist regimes that I had foreseen and which I'm told is the happy crumbling of an idea of man and of society that could never have been anything but the inhumane harbinger of such a collapse. According to this view, my life has been not just one long mistake, but a guilty

---

5 A town in the small island of San Pietro a handful of kilometres off the coast of Sardinia. In Summer 1975, it was the location of the first 'feminist holiday'—a meeting of 200 or so women promoted by Melandri, among others. See Lea Melandri, '1975: il '68 delle donne' in '70. *Gli anni in cui il future incominciò*, supplement no. 6 to *Liberazione* (March 2007): 42–4. [Trans.]

one: I was a disciple of inhumanity. Do the graves of Timişoara not rise up before my eyes?[6]

I know all too well that by the time this issue of *Lapis* comes out, we will have stopped talking about it. Perhaps a reader will think to herself: 'Timişoara, what does this strange word make me think of?' because in the world of information (which imposes itself upon us as reality itself) something else will occupy the stage. And so, my dear women, my friends, can critically shake their heads and say, 'But don't you see for yourself how your famous reality eats itself up, forgets itself? In what futile game are you asking us to take part? You harassed *Orsa Minore* first with Vietnam and then with Danzig: who even talks about these things any more? We were right when we said we didn't want to deal with them.' The temporality of information proves them right and, truth be told, I am no lover of information.

But I do not want to divide myself in two any longer.

I no longer have the strength to strive for the unity of two distant orbits. They live within me in all their distance, and I suffer them as such. Perhaps one day I'll

---

6 The Romanian town in which the 1989 Revolution began, sparked by protests of the Hungarian minority. News of the deaths of thousands in a supposed massacre in the town circulated in December 1989 was later debunked, and the mass graves revealed as a hoax. [Trans.]

know how to find the link, the connection. For now,
however, I know I no longer want to (and, it being the
time for new year's resolutions, never again will) go and
speak somewhere about women's emotions or tempo-
ralities, or about 'women and . . .' (unless it's about
abortion or sexual violence, matters about which I have
still not understood if the 'real' women speak or not,
but about which I would like a few lines of legislation
from Parliament and no more speeches, because I am
even more intolerant than most of the ethical–psycho-
logical theses of politicians on femininity and sex). At
the end of my 'feminine' meetings, there is always a
woman who comes up to me and urges I continue to
write about the whole world, implying that she herself
could not. 'Real' women look with affection upon my
role as the androgynous friend, because every now and
again I put some man in the corner, charging him like
Saint George hurtling at the belly of the dragon, wav-
ing the banner of my sex. But they think of me as a
'one-off'. And so it is implicitly understood that if I turn
up here or there, invited by this or that women's group,
I always leave behind something or other that is trou-
bling me, like an umbrella forgotten in the cloakroom:
Tiananmen or the fate of communists or, God forbid,
Martin Heidegger and whether one can be both a Nazi
and a great philosopher. Isn't this simply schizophrenia?
Yes it is. With its related sufferings and muteness. You'll
say to me: 'But doesn't it trouble you that, when you

go and speak about these questions in men's meetings, you leave yourself as a woman at the door?' Because men are accustomed to compartmentalizing lives in a way that women tell me they do not want to do, and when I speak with men, it's clear that 'other' things might be at stake. Women, instead, force a choice upon me: it's either this or that.

And today they tell me: 'Why do you remain silent about the time of women, on their need to return to the great paradigms in order to decipher them? On their need to discover the scene they are reliving and in which they are caught and which may perhaps destroy them? Didn't this also happen to you?'. In this case I can only respond that I remain silent because I will only speak if doing so will provide them more illumination, not less. Something that will let me see everything better, instead of telling me that most of what I experience is somehow parenthetical to my being a woman. Today it is described to me as 'parenthetical' even from the side 'history', that of men. I stand accused. I cannot bring myself to recant. Everything that is happening is but a painful confirmation of my convictions. I don't know if I can explain this, and how and to whom and why, going to the roots—or indeed whether I should keep quiet or continue with daily life as always: which, as far as what troubles me is concerned, means more or less staying quiet. When it comes to this question, I stand alone. I don't know which women I can speak to about it. And if I turn away from the big questions and towards the daily particulars and ask myself, for example, whether the mass graves in Timişoara really do exist, whether the graves might be medical rather than 'political'—as it seems from the signs of autopsies—and what kind of hospital throws bodies into the ground, and whether someone had dug them up to incite not only terror but revolt, or if perhaps the terror was so widespread that no one manipulated anything, but many nevertheless saw what was not there? Who among the women-women will descend with me into these questions that propel me back into the meaning of my craft? And with whom can I talk about what moves a people, what match lights a fire? And why some people take to the streets and others stay at home? What is an old communist?

I do not have any space within me, now, at the end of 1989, except for the (not unforeseen) magnitude of this question. Nothing has taken me by surprise, but an expected death is a death all the same, even if it's desired. Opening up an abscess, though a condition for healing, still hurts. The wounds of healing are today emotional and ambiguous, as elementary as the motions of a child. These are the beautiful hours of freedom that tomorrow will send you back to all the old questions; this time around the greatest question is if there is truly no other choice than to live under the laws of money and inequality—not 'diversity' but 'inequality' between those who have and those who don't, those who can and those who can't, and the rules of a democracy that separates you from politics, or instead to fall under the tyranny of a system entirely in the hands of men and thus entirely at the mercy of their whims and ambitions. What is worse: the rule of man or woman, or that of money? That of man or woman, they naturally cry out. People who have lived lives like mine now rally beneath this slogan, lamenting how hope turned into horror. Not only are the tyrannies dead, so too is the legitimacy of wanting a more equal and just society. The hopes you have nurtured—they tell us—are criminal hopes. As soon as I rejoice at the sight of the faces around the rubble of the Berlin Wall, I am sent back to a kind of before-and-after, as if everything that is happening does so against the meaning that I have given to my (not so few) years on this earth.

The collapse of a doctrine to which I too have fallen victim is thrown back at me as if I were one of the guilty, and in a certain sense I am. I am asked to think about something else. To pass over to the other side because my own has too many skeletons in its closet, so many that are yet to be disinterred. 'You are tired,' you will tell me. 'It was obvious. It'll be good for you. Don't think that you're the only one who has been taken aback by what has happened. Now you've lost your totalizing manias, your living as a man while being a woman, and thinking as a man/woman. You'll never be free of the furies that bite at your heels as long you want to understand everything. Just be a woman: extraneous, partial. Distance yourself from the other within you.' The other? But I am not two, I am only one.

5

ON THE THRESHOLD OF MYSTERY*

Among the many forms of knowledge that feminist movements lay claim to—in opposition to male abstraction or *logos*—is the 'knowledge of the body'. They invoke the experience of maternity, in which the body is double and for a long time becomes the 'other', the child, who remains physically and psychically bound to the mother; but also the practice of caring for the sick, through an awareness of 'simple' remedies that women have passed down over the centuries—to the extent of feeling themselves endowed with special powers and persecuted like witches. Some writings, such as the works of Trota of Salerno[1] on women's illnesses, supposedly confirm women's heritage of

---

* Published in *Lapis. Percorsi della riflessione femminile*, 8 June 1990.

1 A twelfth-century Southern Italian medical practitioner, associated with early treatises on obstetrics and gynaecology, such as *De curis mulierum* (On Treatments for Women). [Trans.]

corporeal knowledge, material to be found in the past and recuperated for today. But is this really the case? Is there really 'female knowledge' in the strong sense of the term, beyond the relativizing thesis? That is, the thesis, established under the banner of the human sciences, according to which all knowledge, including the most elementary form rejected by modern science, is strong because it has 'its own' area and logic, autonomous and differentiated from other areas and logics. Long before Carlo Ginzburg's 'evidential paradigm',[2] Wittgenstein's remarks on Frazer's *The Golden Bough*,[3] took revenge, as it were, on behalf of the entirety of 'savage thought' against modern scientific reductionism.

But if savage thought is indeed a kind of thought, the fact remains that past female thought and experience has not taken place within a closed realm—as may be said of savage culture—but in parallel with another culture for which it frequently acts as a sounding board and from which it borrows certain frameworks. It has accordingly presented itself in recent years as an

---

2 Carlo Ginzburg, 'Spie. Radici di un paradigma indiziario' in Aldo Gargani (ed.), *Crisi della ragione. Nuovi modelli nel rapporto tra sapere e attività umane* (Turin: Einaudi, 1979). [In English: 'Clues: Roots of a Scientific Paradigm', *Theory and Society* 7(3) (May 1979): 273–88.—Trans.]

3 Ludwig Wittgenstein, 'Remarks on Frazer's *The Golden Bough*' in *The Mythology in Our Language: Remarks on Frazer's Golden Bough* (Giovanni da Col ed. and Stephan Palmié ed. and trans.) (Chicago: Hau, 2018), pp. 29–73.

autonomous mode of thinking, in the sense that it emphasizes the concrete, a 'direct connection' rather than an abstract one, contact with the individual by contrast with the seriality of knowledge and scientific therapy. The fact remains, valid for both anthropological relativism and the contemporary paradigm of knowledge, that one is more easily cured from pneumonia with penicillin than without. And putting an end to the most common cause of female deaths—childbirth—depends on asepsis and antibiotics.[4] The debate between the benefits of alternative and scientific medicine will continue until a holistic vision of 'medical activity' and 'care' is attained, one that could include both. One cannot say, however, that female knowledge of the body is explicitly included within 'alternative medicine'. It is argued that it is a total knowledge stemming from a particular perception of the body, a knowledge that women would possess more than men. By now, this is a truth widely acknowledged, to the extent that, with the exception of doctors themselves, men willingly accept and repeat the claim—a 'coda' to the maternal role they happily recognize, a biological and social role

---

4 Edward Shorter, *A History of Women's Bodies* (New York: Basic Books, 1982). Shorter's study considers the feminist polemic pertaining to 'knowledge about birth' which is meant to demonstrate the superiority of the historical midwife, the *sage femme* of the village, in relation to births handled by doctors. In truth, the variation in results and the decline in the mortality rate happened in the current century; first with sterilized surfaces and then with antibiotics after the Second World War.

admitted without further discussion, along with all the obligations and limitations that accompany it.

But this specific female perception of the body, direct and immediate, does not seem so certain. Even the 'anarchic need for motherhood', to use an apt expression recently coined by Natalia Ginzburg,[5] is not experienced without trauma, uncertainty and contradictions. When we listen to women who have the mental freedom to analyse themselves—for example, during pregnancy—the sound we hear is far from clear and united, as previous issues of *Lapis* have documented.

And once one pays attention to the course of a woman's life, one perceives the symbolic compulsion operating between a woman and her body, including beyond maternity—a determining weight when it comes to her self-perception or her ideas about what she might do with her potential destiny. This is a largely symbolic, indirect and received perception. It tends to replace a 'knowledge' of the body with a perception, a 'model of the body', one exterior to immediate experience and tending to become an experience in itself. This is not 'knowledge' but a dense and dramatic 'fantasy'.

I hold between my hands an intellectual biography of Greta Garbo,[6] a female icon of the first half of the

---

5 Natalia Ginzburg, *Serena Cruz o la vera giustizia* (Turin: Einaudi, 1990).

6 Alexander Walker, *Garbo: A Portrait* (London: Sphere Books, 1982).

century, just as Marilyn Monroe was for most of the second half. Greta however was even more of an icon, thanks to the unironic investment that she (and Hollywood) made in her body—the body of a Goddess no doubt, but also a fated one. When Lubitsch and then Cukor made her into a woman who laughs and makes others laugh, the end had been reached: people rejected the change, and at thirty-six, Greta Garbo left the cinema and spent the rest of her life in seclusion.[7] The few non-studio photographs (which had been taken exclusively by Cecil Beaton with the aid of a specialized camera) that were made when she was in her forties show her as older than she really was—a manifestly unaccepted face—and a sharp, masculine body, the languor and stage clothes now absent. No woman who has lived a public life has received from the image that the public returned to her such a tragic conditioning. Her true life, a world of relations, lasted less than eighteen years: the period of her brilliant youth and of the possibility for the cameraman to place a torch in her bosom for the close-ups, in order to illuminate that marvel of marble skin, the shape of her eyes and mouth above her twisted neck (the result of a spinal defect)—without that light giving any sign of the passing of time. When this ageing finally did emerge in Cukor's film, as the

---

7 The reference is to the directors of Garbo's last films, *Ninotchka* (1939) and *Two-Faced Woman* (1941), both comedies. [Trans.]

beautiful maturity of a thirty-something woman and the shift from tragedy to comedy—in which seduction reveals its ironic, laughable aspect—Garbo was rejected. And she rejected herself, she ran away, and no one ever saw her again. This is an extreme case. But there were very few women from her generation (she was born in 1905) who would continue their careers on stage while undergoing—that is, tolerating—their own ageing. Barbara Stanwyck and Katharine Hepburn, only a little younger, are two examples, women who used their image from a certain distance, working more in comedy than drama, thus drawing on the effects of a charm that is not exclusively derived from the body. Yet for the most part the latter is what is imposed, it is what possesses value. Here the body is essentially the face: eroticism—paradoxically thanks to Hollywood's puritan Hays Code—found far more subtle directions in   the face and gestures than in the unbuttoned shirt, the revealed lingerie and the clutching of bodies (an extraordinary step was Rita Hayworth's famous stripped-off glove, in that long black dress). But a face thus emphasized brings with it a preferential, impeccable and even rigid image. Thanks to the close-up, the cinema became the greatest worshipper of the female body but also the most ruthless architect of its fixed, invariable image.

The female prototype of early cinema has become the imperative for Western women, an inaccessible perfection shifted onto screens, newspapers and calendars, destined to impose feelings of inadequacy: too fat, too thin, too pimply, hair too dull and so on, with all the melancholies suffered by young women who grew up between the 1930s and the 1960s. The prototype would be broken in the 1960s and the irruption of a transgressive subjectivity, one that also shattered Hollywood's beauty codes. The exemplar became more complex and less elitist. All the same, it is doubtful that this different imaginary came closer to the female perception of the body, to a conscious agreement with it, or indeed, to knowledge of the body itself.

In truth, knowledge of the body does *not* accompany the daily life of man and woman. While being the closest, the body is also the least frequented zone of understanding. To explain why, one must turn to psychoanalysis and modern psychiatry. I will limit myself here to claiming that knowledge of the body, even though it logically ought to be the first and most interesting object of exploration, has always been quasi-magically off-limits. The body is born, grows old and dies and we are born, grow old and die with it: *with*, as if it were something other than ourselves. Raise your hands, all those who would not have spoken in this way.

We perceive the body, if not as an encasement, as a 'mode' of our being. Even though we know full well that we do not exist without it, we experience it as something internal / external. We grow old, we get ill, we unfortunately die: it is the body that drags us along to its own rhythms, plans and disasters. The arrival of puberty disturbs us, menopause overturns us. The sense of extraneity or, reciprocally, of being 'filled', of which women are more conscious during maternity, is testimony to this impossibility of *immediately* taking on a female, biological specificity—which logically ought to be as concrete and unnoticeable as breathing. Even the less dramatic and totalizing functions of the body are received as a command arriving from something external, sent to our 'inner life': our body has hunger, it feels cold. It gets tired. We feed *it*, we warm it up, we let it rest. In sleep and sex we seem to escape death because in these states we are absorbed within the body, an experience that remains anomalous with regard to the normal state of consciousness. As for consciousness itself, reasoning tells us that this is a function of the body, primarily of the brain, and not the other way round. But of course we do not perceive it as such at all.

This is partly because we do not know anything about the body as a whole organism. We only have some idea of its externality, its shell, that which we see, and a little about its superficial functions: pain, cold, hunger. Even sex is shadowy. When sick, we are certain that there is something 'external' that has penetrated us, to the extent that the current idolization of prevention views the man or woman who has allowed themselves to be penetrated as almost guilty of a lack of care. The few diseases that we catch so treacherously are themselves connected to social flaws (the equation 'AIDS = individual transgression' finds its collective double in the equation 'cancer = industrial society'). Treatment understood as a 'disease-hunt' is the consequence of this simplification of our materiality, conceived of as integral but potentially undermined by, and thus also liberated from, an evil incursion. Not even the by-now relatively widespread idea of the existence of an immune system, or that of a genetic code, has managed to shake off the immediacy of this crude perception, which both forges and breaks the shackles of the body, our exposed and fragile aspect. As for the rest, if we're not doctors, what do we know of anatomy and basic physiology? Medically speaking, even an educated man or woman knows nothing at all. They learn as little as possible. They're readier to delve into the psyche than 'within the shell' or beyond the skin. The orifices, the mouth, the vagina, the anus are perceived as a limit point, an atrium, a threshold of mystery. A negative and vaguely repulsive mystery. The only time I've been in an operating theatre to observe a desperate intervention on a friend, I was astonished—once the scalpel had opened the abdomen under her breast down to the pubic area and the edges of the incision had been pulled back—by the appearance of a wonderful square of blue, pink and lilac, carefully composed and veiled, the

vermillion blood perfectly blocked by ligaments or channelled through a system of transfusion. With amaze-
ment I remembered my frankly horrible anatomy
atlases, which perhaps for the sake of simplification
harden the colours and hues: in truth the internal body
is extremely beautiful, pulsating, tender in all its forms
and hues. Is it simply out of love that none of my
friend's family dared to observe this extreme situation?
I wore the green gown and mask as requested of me
by an enraged surgeon who imposed them on me
saying 'Let's try not to faint or vomit'.

Along with this paradoxical not knowing, which
betrays a primordial ban, we can observe the different
perceptions of the bodies of the two sexes, stemming
from different social and biological roles.

Man too is subject to the servitude of the imaginary, but before beauty—ambiguously defined for
him by contrast to his feminine counterpart—comes
strength and 'the ability to work', at first with the hand
and then (in keeping with the gradual transformation
of labour) with technological prostheses to the hand
and the cerebral functions inherent to activity, memory,
speed, connection. Aside from this, man is also subject
to the imperative of 'strength' in his sexuality, put to
the test in the erection, the guarantee of an always-
threatened virility, constantly at risk of failure. Woman
is less subject to the symbolism/servitude of strength
and activity. Even if she has slaved and laboured for

millennia, in the imaginary or the symbolic she is not defined by her activity—which is regarded as historical and contingent—but by her 'appearance' in eternal functions such as maternity and seduction. The former is sacred and sacrificial, the latter (at least in patriarchal society) is her specific power and, to a certain extent, dangerous for man, himself being secondarily seductive, if at all. For woman, being seductive is so inherent that appearance becomes a decisive factor: she is, above all, 'seen'. A mirror constantly accompanies her: man's staring at her body, for whom she is first and foremost either beautiful or ugly, blonde or brunette, legs and breasts and waists. She cannot but see herself seen. Women who behave as if this were not the case are deemed frigid, self-deniers. And they are few and far between. We are so accustomed to caring for our appearance that it seems eccentric to not do so. And we know that the message we transmit with our appearance does not in the first place reveal our social status, but our body, emphasized by our dress and make-up. And any deformation, or simply the ageing that brings deformation, is a cause for disgust, a wound, an ugly degeneration—far more for us than for man. The judgement of a woman's standing, even in her own eyes, is a form of cruelty: I dress 'for myself', I apply make-up for myself. Woman is beauty. No doubt this is also a claim to autonomy. But the word is not chosen accidentally: beauty pertains to woman in the sense that if she is not beautiful, she is not a woman. Or she needs to be an extraordinarily superior woman, and even in this case one says 'despite'. Unlike for men, for her the canon remains obligatory. Our perception of the body, aside from all the initial prohibitions, must also pass through a dense cultural membrane. If neither man nor woman 'knows' the body (or knows far less than any other given present or proximate subject), we probably know even less about the female body than the male one, due to a screen formed by the image/model imposed on women in all civilizations, focusing on her sexual role. To that extent, this self-image—unlike its masculine equivalent, which manifests itself in multiple ways—shares with sex its darkness and danger, its extreme nature as a moment of acceptance or refusal, as a limit-experience. (The well-meaning 'sexual libera-tion' attempts, somewhat naively, to domesticate this within a technics of satisfaction, with a reduced emo-tional impact. This is yet again a male suggestion, and who knows how truthful: making love makes one feel good, no different than a fresh-squeezed orange juice for the parched, only with a little more affect, etc.).[8] The need to confront this reactionary image, this seeing oneself seen, complicates the female relation to the body, compounding the symbolic charge of maternity; they are the two plates of armour that further weigh

8 Stefania Giorgi and Roberta Tatafiore (eds), *Le nuove amanti*: *Storia di sesso e amore oggi* (Trento: Noi Donne-Lyra Libri, 1989).

down on the 'shell'. Importantly, for a woman this also works in the strict sense of the term, weighing down on the skin: her precious, milky, rosy, golden but unwaveringly smooth perimeter. What horror, the illnesses that affect this peel. They make us tremble inside with the fear of something other than death; there are illnesses that are more serious but also more tolerable than those that cause an external devastation. They can even be graceful (pallidness, the blue veins of the breast, the weak bones of the wrist harbour centuries of seduction). The pre-eminence of appearance even conditions one's perception of those functions by which the body feeds, empties and moves itself, how it walks, runs, sleeps, feels 'other bodies', a feeling that is problematic even outside of the sexual relation.

One can pass one's entire life without perceiving anything other than this fabric of received images, stratified and interwoven with direct but hidden perceptions—all while 'caring for oneself' and for others. But it is a slim basis for 'knowledge'. Rather, it represents a sediment of praxis, of experiences with a deeply codified meaning, and an expanse of uninterrogated emotions: to content oneself with this is not a sign of independence but tends towards a limitation of those (for the most part unspoken) variations by which the 'body's code' is experienced or endured. If one adds to this the recent beginnings of a feminist development of the psychoanalysts' return to the relation between the psyche and the body, and some of the early attempts by modern neurology (noted by Freud with some discomfort) in the direction of the elementary perceptions of the corporeal self that are contained within the right cerebral hemisphere—the perception of the self in space, the visual apperception of the totality of the image, etc.[9]—then I can conclude, on a provisional basis, that female 'knowledges' are not 'of the body'; rather, they are knowledges of a praxis—partly social, partly personal, greatly overdetermined and extremely emotive—of this object that remains the most ambiguous element of our experience.

9 Oliver Sacks, *The Man Who Mistook His Wife for a Hat and Other Clinical Tales* (New York: Harper & Row, 1970).

6

RAISE THE RED LANTERN*

A building surrounded by a wall, with wings that enclose the windowless stone courtyards. High up above, a lone compartment where those condemned to death are executed. The daily morning call, the meals taken together. No personal objects, strict discipline. What might it be? Either a prison or a convent.

Instead, it is the beautiful aristocratic Chinese house of *Raise the Red Lantern*. The director, Zhang Yimou, has provided it with perfect proportions, the stone nicely smoothed and the tiled roofs harmoniously inclined like the curled ends of a pair of slippers. This is where the First, Second, Third and Fourth Mistresses live, served by women and controlled by men, each in her own accommodation, robed in silk, their faces smoothed with make-up. The spatial

* Published in *Lapis. Percorsi della riflessione femminile*, 16 June 1992.

symmetry encloses the bodies in their robes, bodies neither exposed nor fragmented; there is nothing natural
here, whether animal or plant. The director's camera,
always set on a frontal plane, underlines this rigidity.

The film has been described as icy and aestheticiz-
ing. To me it appeared violent and disturbing. The
building that hosted the roles played out within it man-
ages to amalgamate harmony and constriction. Its
perfect form is closed and claustrophobic; it encases
the individual within the repetition of gestures and
behaviours, outside of which stands only transgression
and death. Inscribing in all the physical spaces, this
form displays the lives of women who, in the 1920s,
have decided to be chosen by a rich man. *Wives and
Concubines*, in the book's original title. The West has
narrated 'property' over women, but not this total
objectification: it is the hyperbole of woman's archety-
pal condition. Perhaps this is what makes the film
almost intolerable. The female student (that is, an
emancipated woman) who crosses the threshold in a
skirt and blouse, her plaits on her shoulders and lug-
gage in hand, is not received with any kind of gesture
that might denote a relationship, other than with a mistress or guest. She is taken by servants to her room,
washed, reclothed in silk, her hair combed and the soles
of her feet massaged to be sexually adequate for the
man who has chosen her and whom she will see only
once she is in bed. There is no ceremony either before

or afterwards. The following morning the four women and their four servants, perfectly clothed at the gateway, find out together with whom the master will spend the following night, and the red lantern is brought to the courtyard of the chosen one, to be lit while he is with her—not a sign of love, but of selection.

During the day, the men leave to partake in life, while the women visit each other and move within select parts of the building. They do nothing; they simply wait. The young student has neither books nor the flute given to her by her father—these have been confiscated. The camera follows her, but it does not follow her gaze when she looks out from the high terraces. Nor does it follow her beyond the bedroom curtain, where she carries out the sexual requests made of her. In the West, a margin of reciprocal seduction remains in the game of love, in which hierarchies can momentarily be recomposed, and in which the desire, need, tension between two people can creep in. The film suggests that matters are different here, thus there is nothing to narrate. The camera does not even show his face. This man does not exist other than to command. The only needs are his own and the concubine's only role is to satisfy them. Beyond the bed curtain, she ceases to exist. And how does she exist the rest of the time? Solitary, on her guard, uncomfortable: because the four women live out his power as a shadow within themselves, to the extent that they are preferred for their greater sexual service and, even better, for being mothers of sons. These two levels change the order of authority/age: the First Mistress, almost ossified, has a grown-up son; the Second only managed to give birth to a baby girl, and on the same day the Third gave birth to a son. The young student, the Fourth Mistress, thus represents a threat to the Second. She feigns a pregnancy and, once discovered, reveals in her anger that the Third Mistress is having an affair with the doctor. Later, from the silence of her abode, she sees a group of men in black from far off carrying a white bundle, debating desperately among themselves in the isolated room on the terrace, where one day she had found a pair of rotten silk shoes on the ground, the possessions of an unknown owner. We do not see the men hang the Third Mistress, we only see them enter and exit as though in flight.

The Fourth Mistress is the only voice who screams without tiring from her room: 'Murderers, murderers, murderers.' She will be defined as—and indeed, perhaps she has become—mad. In order to speak about women, Zhang Yimou thus speaks about an absolute and annihilating power. Or, conversely, to speak about power he speaks about those who are entirely objectified by it, women. It is not so in *Red Sorghum* and *Ju Dou*: in these films the protagonist is an object of violence but also partially frees herself through passion and, in doing so, rules herself—even if at the price of blood and revolt. In *Red Sorghum*, set during the war with Japan, the protagonist's freedom coincides with that of the Chinese people, while in the films set in the 1920s it seems to correspond with their oppression. And yet Zhang Yimou never talks about politics nor power. Power expresses itself through negation, through the prohibitions that target those subject to it, for whom no other moves are possible—as in a game of checkers— other than those already established for the sake of reciprocal control.

The student's error lies in thinking that something is in her power, that she can act. But the only variation allowed is a modification within the hierarchies between the four women and, of course, the servants, all at the master's pleasure. This form of relationship does not provide space for jealousy—which implies a feeling— but only envy, accompanying the 'social' insecurity of the house, precluding any and every kind of solidarity: more generally, it precludes every free relation. One can see a slim thread of desire (another lost good) on the day in which the Fourth Mistress meets the oldest son playing a flute on the other side of the room. They share a silence and a glance that speaks of an impossible meeting. But there is nothing more, because the son is also the property of his father—which is why the camera rests on his face—and the only time we see him speak to the woman is to admonish her for having attempted to feign pregnancy: 'You were stupid.'

And she was. She thinks she can remove herself from the rules that the others already knew from long experience, just as they know its interstices. The Second Mistress, who comes from the world of the theatre, knows the limits within which she is allowed to sing, play and flirt with the doctor. It is the protagonist, instead, who makes the greatest error: in the admonishing silence of the other women, she requests that her servant be ferociously punished for having lit red lanterns in her room to pretend to be in the position of her mistress, a position that she will never hold. How can she not realize that she is at the mercy of the humiliated young woman?

The servant denounces the false pregnancy as soon as a bloodied undergarment falls into her hands. And her Mistress, believing that she is taking revenge on the doctor, brings about the death of her friend. Perhaps she envied her. She doesn't know. We are beyond conscious choices by now.

The absolutely unfree wreak havoc on one other. There is no escape, Zhang Yimou tells us. A story of women. The most educated of the four, who believed she could maintain some grip over her situation, discovers her own powerlessness. Perhaps this is why she goes mad.

7

THIS BODY THAT INHABITS ME*

A torrid Friday in a left-wing club in Trastevere. The subject: Women and Work. Very orthodox Marxists and very orthodox feminists. While some man holds forth on Toyotism, a woman bursts out with: 'Begin from your body!' Flummoxed, he responds: 'But the body is an abstraction!' Howling, Babel. I leave a few minutes later.

The body, an abstraction. Only a male professor could come up with such a joke. Is there anything more concrete? Since the dawn of time the body has been material: concrete, tangible, visible matter. The very first material that each person has to hand. It is so definitively terrestrial and perishable that it is always paired with the ungraspable and (one hopes) eternal soul. Body and soul, soma and psyche, spirit and matter.

---

* Published in *Lapis. Percorsi della riflessione femminile*, 23 September 1994.

The atheist and the materialist leave the soul behind, but we are in our bodies, that much is clear. Less clear is at what point the body's materiality becomes 'immaterial matter', such as cerebral processes or, worse still, psychic ones. For some time now, the experts tell us that this or that part of the brain (well-defined in the anatomy books) emits 'information'—a conveniently ambiguous word spanning materiality and spirituality—that tells some other part (again well-defined) to do this or that. 'Sleep now!' it says, and the body goes to sleep. Whatever, I'll let it go—physiology is not my concern here. Let's start from myself and how I perceive 'my' body. I will admit that one might say 'my' about something that 'I am' and which 'is' myself. Because there can be no doubt that 'I am' my body but that I perceive it/myself as an 'other', even if it is the closest other, indeed a clinging one. I am inside it (where else, otherwise?) but in some way 'I feel' that I'm outside it. Just as when my eyes see a slice of me within their radius, they see my feet but my feet cannot see them. Without a mirror, I feel both outside myself and attached from the inside, so that I cannot see my entire body. I would say that, fundamentally, I miss it. With a mirror—that is to say, through an object—I can see that which otherwise I cannot see, and with two mirrors set opposite one other, I can see all of me. But with one mirror alone, I see a disorderly version of myself, and with two an infinite multiplication. There is something bizarre about the sensation of this damned body. It is from the body of others that I truly understand how I look and how I move, by which means 'my' body is transmitted through another's, a body that certainly is not my own and certainly is not me, but that 'I' see and, in a certain sense, understand more about than mine. I can touch it more than my own. It must be because of the mirror that I am always surprised by photographs, in which everything is somehow and indefinably different: they show how I am seen and not how I see me. 'That's exactly like you', someone assures me. When I say: 'I like this one, but not this one,' is it perhaps because the former reminds me more of what I've seen in the mirror? Or because it is more similar to an image of my body that I've made for myself, measuring it against a body that is not my own?

From every angle, this body that inhabits me and that I inhabit escapes from and returns to me, as if it were the eel of my consciousness, an eel attached to 'me'.

Miles and miles of bibliographies have been written on the perception of one's own body. But as I am quite intent this time around on beginning from myself, I will not even take a glance at the bibliography. Finding myself within, together with and inside this body in 1994, I assume that what I call 'consciousness' is an emitting-and-receiving system that has a certain location in the head but extends throughout the body and ends at its borders. Somewhat like my computer. If I take a hammer to my computer, its brain will spill out of the innumerable wires. Is a corpse a smashed computer, or one without batteries or electricity? Or is it sleeping? Death and exhaustion. That might be the case. Without a doubt I have been programmed so as to have a perception of my body as myself/other. From as far back as I can recall, everyone did everything they could to confuse me. My mother said: 'Move yourself' not 'Move your legs', although at times she said 'Your hand', 'your leg', 'your arse', 'your hair' and 'your stomach' (this is, I think, the only internal body part that one mentions to children, in relation to eating: 'Don't go swimming on a full stomach', 'you've got an empty stomach').

And then there was my sister Mimma, who was visibly different from me by dint of her weight, hair and eyes: 'Don't hurt Mimma!' But 'Mimma's hands', 'Mimma's hair' not 'Mimma hands', 'Mimma hair', 'Mimma body'. She too was twain. Moreover, the word 'body' itself was one you heard very rarely, if not as 'parts of the body'. Which are not quite as important. We did not talk about the shit and piss we emitted, but soon enough I knew that, like food, this was not mine, that it came from outside and I gave it back, albeit in an unpleasurable way. Like the timber in the stove that turns to ash, the product was heat itself and I am more or less heat.

Outside and inside is clear enough to me even when in fact it is far from clear; the heat and cold come from outside. The flu and the common cold come from outside too, microbes like tiny mosquitoes whose incursion must be impeded. If I graze a knee this means that I have knocked against an outside, the same as if I fall from the loquat tree: I sort myself out and I don't have to tell my mother, who had said to me: 'Go on, but don't come complaining if you hurt yourself.' Indeed, it's worse if you tear your shirt rather than your knee, as the latter doesn't sort itself out. Then there was the time when I dislocated my wrist and had to confess (my mother did not shout at me—if the body could not sort itself out, I was absolved).

Between outside and inside lies the zone of pleasure and pain, and not only physical pain. I created a system, I 'reasoned through' matters, as my friends might say.

The relation between myself and my body is much less clear. When is that demon truly me? When I was younger, a child was an adult in making. Every month you measured your height against the edge of a doorway marked with pins, and thus I was and was not, because I was *work in progress*, and one fine day I would be. The body would acquire the correct size and form that was my due. I was in a hurry to have it because it meant being able to be and do certain things: I don't understand those childhoods that don't harbour a yearning for growth. My own childhood was not an unhappy one, but I was in a waiting room. I recall the finish line of seventeen: finally, I was there. I don't know why seventeen instead of eighteen—I would need an analyst for that. I know that I looked at myself and knew I had been menstruating since I was twelve—I was no sylph, I had arrived. I said to myself: Here we are and, more or less, here we shall remain. But it was clear that I would not change much and that there was little choice but to be content with myself, with this body. It was no catastrophe: the legs were almost straight, a decent height, same for the weight. But I was *not* how I wanted to/had to be, the diva of the 1930s, like Garbo or Stanwych. I was not long and supple (the word 'supple' has always enchanted me as far as bodies are concerned, like the word *chatoyant* for fabrics). The danger of always being not long-limbed enough and too distant from suppleness has always pursued me, to this day: I have always observed myself. I am not disciplined, I do not know how to follow a diet, I'm too lazy for athletic exercise. By 'observed' I mean 'watched with suspicion and alarm. I ought to eat less, move more, not wear those kinds of clothes'. I suppose that if I seem somehow acceptable by now—considering my age and the fact that at first glance one does not see the curved spine or the hump at the base of my neck—then this constant state of alarm must have functioned as a form of athletics. Furthermore, I was neither brunette nor blonde nor redhead, but greenish. A terrible head of hair, hard and straight instead of full and wavy. (Thanks to Greta Garbo's appearance in *Queen Christina*, I had a model to try and imitate . . .). My sister Mimma used to have silky black hair. In the end my face would have been judged neither beautiful nor ugly had I not had a large and strange mole, badly placed. I've always hated it, but never had it removed; I have exactly the same relation to it as Georgina in Hawthorne's short story.[1] A negative sign.

It is all very well for some to say: 'Don't bother me, I'm happy with my body.' I look at Claudia Schiffer and think to myself: who knows how she lives like this, perfectly within herself. I don't believe that fat is beautiful. Tosh. And I have nothing against facelifts and all kinds of adjustments, so long as they don't cost a fortune. I would gladly remove some of my tummy but then I forget about it (is that possible?). Without doubt I see myself with a clear 'form', with regards to which I think 'there's too little there, too much over here'. This experience of form does not seem strange to me: we are programmed to provide everything with a form, so why should we not also give one to ourselves? Certainly, we women depend on the form that the other sex prefers for us. We are thoroughly observed and measured. But this would also be the case if we were

---

1 A reference to Nathaniel Hawthorne's *The Birth-Mark* (1843) in *The Complete Short Stories of Nathaniel Hawthorne* (Garden City, NY: Doubleday, 1959), pp. 227–37. [Trans.]

Amazons. Whether masculine or feminine, we all have 'beautiful' forms in mind, and many of these forms are only occasionally discovered; indeed, they're extremely rare (we rejoice when we find them in crystals or the orbits of the stars or in the flight of birds). The simplifications of raw nature disturb us. There are 'forms' for the male and female body that perhaps have variations, but only over slow waves, lasting centuries. I think I've seen nothing that fits this notion of form better than the masculine torsos in the Parthenon Museum one morning, the light shining down across those imperceptible variations from shoulder to waist. And the female body seems to me perfect in some such statues, gathered in themselves and only slightly undulating (supple). I find the Greeks fascinating for this. In Indian paintings and sculptures the female figures seem to be in danger, their breasts and waists overflowing—ever in danger of not being at all. And then Chinese and Japanese, women appear transitory, ghostly bodies of man, foldable into his own, functioning for his sexuality. Greek bodies seem durable, they are in themselves. If I had to choose: 'Which body would you like?' I know exactly where I would happily insert myself. This is not to speak of faces: all my models in that department are in the great heights of cinema. But the face matters less; there is too much of a person in a face, and it's not so simple to want another. The body too has its more and less strategic zones. When translating Thomas Mann's

The Black Swan [*Die Betrogene*][2] I could not understand how for him a young girl with a limp was 'out'; for me it is the lack of a hand that makes me perceive a mutilated body. And the skin? Being ill horrifies me, while a fatal disease may be beautiful. The ideal form, the idea of form, is a very strange thing.

So, a body measured by a form than is not my own. And in movement. Aside from the fleeting moment when I was seventeen years old, how did I fare? I once heard Catherine Deneuve respond to the question: 'How does a very beautiful woman live?' with the words: 'She looks in the mirror every morning to spot where the cracks are starting to appear.' As for me, given that I didn't like myself, I was always suspicious—there was always a crack, which meant I was not particularly disturbed by the onset of ageing. I used to examine myself coldly, with a friendly glance: waist, chest, hips, the lines of my arms and legs. They were blurring—this much was clear. For many years they dissatisfied me but without drama; it was foretold. Then there was a shock. Later, ten years ago, by the sea, after a shower and while I lay on the towel, I saw a deep line across my stomach and my waist: a scratch from a rock I told myself. But no scratch, no rock: it was a line, *the* line, the above and below of the body which no longer managed to keep themselves apart, instead falling one

2 Thomas Mann, *L'inganno* (Rossana Rossanda trans.) (Venice: Marsilio, 1992).

on top of the other. This was something quite different from Athena's torso. I recall the time, the place, my horror, my resignation. No changes had occurred as far as the office of vital statistics is concerned but it was a turn I had not foreseen. I had remained 'young' from my thirties through to my sixties, even if my sixties had not been a graceful hurdle. My forties had been cheerful and my fifties only somewhat apprehensive. My sixties were a catastrophe, and that sign said as much. Not the white hair, which came early and helpfully substituted my greenish hue. Not the arthritic back I could not see, or the hump on my neck: it was that line/wrinkle[3] which said I was no longer keeping up. The body ages downwards. This is the moment in which the 'form', however modest it may already have been, moves on.

The body's movement over the years is different from that of illness. I have gone through a deluge of illnesses, the most common ones. But I lived through them in passing; either you die, or they pass. And they passed me by. The deformities of age are different. I look at the hands on the keyboard as I write. They used to be the 'form'. They were beautiful. So beautiful that if someone said to me, 'What beautiful hands you have', I used to reply: 'Yes, they're the most beautiful I've ever seen', a way of cutting the conversation short

---

3 In the original: *riga/ruga* [Trans.]

while also making me an unpleasant witness to the truth. They were the hands of Verrocchio's girl, long and sensitive.[4] It is enjoyable to be a nobody with beautiful hands, a beauty that remains secret to a certain extent: you know it but it doesn't jump out. For some years now, however, these hands have gone to ruin. There is a little knoll at every joint, a small disconnected, irregular bump as if the bone is trying to get out from underneath. On the right index finger, with which I have beaten out millions of words, there is now a kind of distorted mountain. On the back of my hands there are blue veins—I liked them on my mother's— and some brown spots. Never mind. The skin is strange. These hands seem like two tortoises. They are always there, in the middle of things, visible. You cannot forget them. They inform me that my body is on its way out.

It is going. I am not. Yet again, we're not the same. I watch it and I'm furious about what it's doing. Why do the bones move so haphazardly? The doctor tells me, but it feels like he's speaking about someone else. *My* bones! Why is the skin drying out? Why are the fingernails growing dull? How is this going to end? Everything is happening to this dress in which I have been

---

4 Likely a reference to Andrea Del Verrocchio's late-fifteenth-century marble sculpture, *Woman with Flowers* (in Italian: *Gentildonna delle belle mani*, Gentlewoman of the Beautiful Hands), held at the Bargello Museum in Florence, Italy. [Trans.]

inexorably inserted. It is not true that I perceive it. I can only *know* it. Like the fact that I cannot hear from one ear any more, and inside there's a loud noise with a pleasant name: tinnitus. I have tinnitus. A tinnitus has me. A tinnitus has occupied me. It comes from 1952— of course they know everything except how to get rid of it. It's not serious, they say, everyone gets it at your age. When I tell him my age, the doctor's face changes a little. From now on I am back to being sixty-five, otherwise they only get worried if you have something truly terrible. But I will no longer have silence, never. The doctor who took me more seriously put me in a box that seemed like a coffin (and for this reason it was lined with a little sign: 'We're here, you can call us, how are you doing?'), an instrument that whirled around me with a crash; then plates with little skulls came out, a stack of them, as if they had photographed my brain in slices. They did not find a tumour but holes in the white matter. I don't know what white matter is. I knew about the grey kind from Agatha Christie. Isn't it a little creepy? In any case, no one knows what the holes mean, perhaps I always had them, and now the machine can photograph more things than a doctor knows how to read. I don't feel anything and so it's as if they're not there, and perhaps indeed they aren't. If it were serious, I would have some circuit interruptions. My body/myself would warn me in some blunt and drastic manner.

My friends, perhaps you're reading this with some annoyance. The English say it is impolite to speak about one's body; one does not speak of it, you never know what you might bump up against, whether you might hit a nerve—the whole issue has as much emotion as grammar. I have written this because the body is intriguing. The body that one does not perceive is irrelevant. Truly. That which kills you—and sooner or later this befalls all of us—is like a murderer who wanders the streets and when it meets you, shoots. It doesn't pertain to you. So it ought not be read as if it communicated some news. There is no news. The news is there in the ageing, which one lives. You will say to me: 'And why are you talking about the irritation of ageing rather than the problematic, inclusive and disturbing body of your sex?' I suppose because I do not know what to say about being a woman. I simply am one, and I have never managed to take a man seriously *as a man* any more than a woman *as a woman*. And as for the 'practice' of sex (as one says today), I do not know how to speak about it. My generation doesn't know how to and I seriously doubt that the younger one really speaks about it either: cinema, for example, says something about the map of desires but nothing about sex other than as a gymnastic stereotype that works like clockwork every time it isn't a rape. Up till now it has been the word that has disclosed it more than the image. In any case, what would I say? Only that one cannot pass through the whole region of sex without difficulty. I apologize, but I have not traversed it with ease. Has being a woman occupied a central part of my mind? No. In my feelings, pains, desires, anxieties, needs, reassurances, frustrations? Almost. I know all of them in many ways, through many objects—I know passions. That of the union with/abandonment of the other is one such passion. An important one. And now, in the shift from body-me to body-body, is every passion to be extinguished? Perhaps. Some are extinguished, but perhaps the word has little sense. The map of the passions changes along with the topographic chart on which I locate myself: there is more space behind than ahead. I am free to remember, to discover; I am not free to plan, I am free from planning. Time changes, I am less distracted, I think about something I will never see and this no longer pains me: I used to be a ferocious tourist, I used to run so as not to miss anything. I always ran, I continue to run in order to understand—I still have a mountain of things to understand, and it irritates me that I don't understand them. People like me have lived like a piece of the world's mosaic; perhaps it was the war or communism, in any case, it's a wonderful way of living. I have never been bored. When I was sixteen, I used to go to imaginary cemeteries along the lagoon and wail like a troubadour: 'Oh Countess, what is life?' and then an explosion would call me back to an instability much closer to hand. It taught me to appreciate things in the moment, without exaggerating. And I was and remain within other lives, even those far away. Lives that are more decipherable than bodies, come to think of it.

Friends and comrades see me a little like the Nike of Samothrace, driving ahead but with broken wings and without a head. A melancholic, courageous woman. But no. I was never destined for melancholy. I flourish more in tragedy than in melancholy, wailing and shouting. I know the melancholy of being, which is different than that of those who mourn; it is a lacking of vast dimensions, the perception of which is also a kind of having. Or so I believe; I am presumptuous, everyone knows that. I have spread myself everywhere, I have passed through many things, and while there have been moments of weakening, I have not paid an excessive price. These days, I receive signs of love, rarely those of hostility and they rarely concern me anyway. Many questions, many answers. The girl I was is ridiculous but I indulge her. That which is projected onto me (as one says) makes me laugh less—let's be honest, does it really concern me? It does not. If I write my memoirs, I will laugh often. The day the body will send me a message to say: 'Listen, I'm tired, enough now', I hope it will give me time to reply: 'OK. And thank you, I've enjoyed myself greatly.'

Friendship, a Calm Deposit of Self

LEA MELANDRI

In her essay 'Self-Defence of a Political I', which came out in the first issue of the journal *Lapis*, Rossana Rossanda refers to my review of her book *Anche per me*, published by Feltrinelli in the same year. She defines my reading as a loving one, 'close', while also recognizing my 'different' method of establishing the 'I', interiority.

We had met only a few years before, after an exchange/conflict of words—polemical on my part, complimentary on hers—in *il manifesto* but the relation between us was already of the kind that Rossana believed was proper to friendship: an interest in someone, in who they are, an attention to how that person reflects, accepts or rejects us, how they make us think. When she wrote about this in her book, the reference was particularly to the friendship between two women, 'a new, disturbing fact, inasmuch as they can reconstruct a changing identity, one that rebels against the old relations of dependency, whether of the family or the couple.'

Friendship is a relation that assumes a certain autonomy of both parties, a strong structure—either present or possible—of each person's 'I' [...] Passion comes from pathos, from suffering; it is a form of love that confesses it is desperately needy in order to self-heal, to recover from distant wounds, reassure oneself after distant negations, to find a guarantee when it comes to the final question: Do I count enough for someone to be certain that I exist? For someone? No: for that one person from whom the reply can come [. . .] that is passion. Within friendship this terrifying question—whether destructive or healing—simply isn't there. You are friends when the other is taken on and treasured for who they are, and not for that which they give us or for what we demand of them [. . .] How could a woman know friendship? She who only with great difficulty can say she possesses her *own* self, and must put her husband, child or father ahead of herself in the scale of relations? She who was not free to manage either her time or her future? Passion must finish, friendship must last. Thus, the friendship between two women is also the coming together of a self-consciousness that till now has been left in the shadows or rarely spoken of.[1]

The long feminist journey I have gone through leads me to suggest that perhaps the boundaries between love/passion and friendship are not quite so clear, that the power conflict between the sexes, mediated by private life, has unfortunately left its marks on the relation between peers. But it is certainly true that our own friendship, begun as an encounter between different lives and very different political experiences, has accompanied us till today. Indeed, for both of us it has become that 'calm deposit of the self' of which Rossana spoke of once more in her dialogue with Emanuela Fraire on loss and mourning.[2]

As for the book that brought us into contact, it was the title (*Also for Myself: Woman, Person, Memory*) and the preface that attracted me at first. Words that at the time were considered as the substitute for a gesture, the outermost trench of thoughts destined to be lost amid the collective consciousness, were presented here as tools for the transformation of the world, returning to the page in order to describe experiences, feelings, memories, in order to speak about the 'deep and unfathomable waters' that lay behind a body 'hidden away' when it wanted to arrange itself 'on the unmeasurable

---

1 Rossanda, *Anche per me*, pp. 139–41.
2 Emanuela Fraire and Rossana Rossanda, *La perdita* (Lea Melandri ed.) (Turin: Bollati Boringheri, 2008), p. 29.

horizon of history'. And Rossana often returned (including in the pages of *Lapis*) to the 'political apprenticeship' that the war represented for so many of her generation, always with that image of her youthful self in the wax-scented Treasure Room in the Rocchetta Courtyard in Milan, where she made herself 'a kind of Warburg', as the bombing of the city put an end to every 'beautiful private isolation'. The 'path of duty', the categorical imperative that had opened up above her, like the famous starry sky, nevertheless didn't stop her from cultivating beauty within the solitude of knowledge, the love of art, literature, philosophy, cinema and, more generally, the cultural treasure trove trapped for centuries within the 'person', and which feminism was now gradually discovering.

The essays gathered together in Rossana's book responded, on the one hand, to the past—to those 'exquisite things' she would never abandon; on the other, she was replying to women whom she had often met only through the pages of a book, women who made it normal for her to 'tarry with the heart' and even to launch an occasional 'raid' on those areas of thought and sentiment which she had maintained as 'private' for so long. The indiscretion of recounting one's own story having won out—an act that according to her was permitted only to those who possessed the gift of form—she abandoned the impersonal form of writing that belongs to those who consider themselves only a 'speaking segment of a common story'. Rossana admitted that she had begun to see the world in a different way and, 'not without some embarrassment', to confront some questions of feminist politics.

Seen from the horizon of those who had never shied away from attending to biography as well as history, even while keeping them apart, feminism presented itself as the 'germ' of a great act of protest that had been sown within the site of what until that moment had been considered to be a historical 'insignificance'—that is, personal life, the experience of the individual. This meant pushing a weakened politics right up to the final, shadowy, obscure zones of the body's memory.

Within the anomalous practices of the women's movement, Rossana found the 'immense' traces of a condition that cut across individual and species, biology and history, the experience of the individual and social life. But she did so with the impatience of a woman who had seen intolerable pain and injustices rise up from behind the butchery of war, hoping that a feminist revolution 'might bear down into the world with all its weight and dig in like a scalpel to overthrow its course'. In love, as in political struggle, we should have broken unfreedom—hers and his. Responding to the demands of war by becoming a communist, accepting the inescapable, all-encompassing horror that had appeared before her, Rossana defined herself as 'Luciferian' (p. 8

in this volume, hereafter indicated with page numbers in parentheses). But it always seemed to me that she was devilish in urging on a movement right from the start so that it might radically subvert the world in all its complexity.

The 'person' lay at the centre of the intellectual joy of her early studies; now she became aware that its unfathomable depths contained 'the exposed and painful' material represented by woman and the fantasies that man has produced from her.

How exactly had I criticized her so much that, in her first essay for *Lapis*, she felt pushed to provide so heartfelt a defence of her 'political I'? Perhaps due to the fact that she could not manage to see her being a woman before everything else, that she considered replacing the 'battle plan' with the search for the self as a delusion, that she was fascinated by a 'patience in suffering'—one that for me harked back uncomfortably to a feminine self-denial.

Perhaps a little mischievously, I read this within the final pages of the book, those dedicated to Rosa Luxemburg, or rather as she appeared in Margarethe von Trotta's film, *Rosa L.*: Rosa the 'unloved' woman whom women 'have forgotten'. I found much of her in this sketch: 'strength in suffering, steadfastness, the melancholy of history's long arcs'; but also 'a woman of the highest level' for having known how to hold together thought and emotion, passion and reason. I could not but note the extent to which Rossana, consciously or otherwise, recognized herself in one of the final images of the film, when Rosa moves across to Lulu Kautsky and, exhausted, rests her head upon her breast.

Rossana writes:

In the arms and face of the friend who embraces her we see, I think, what Margarethe feels for our distant sister, ripping her away from the heavy negation of feeling that today lies heavy on everything for which she lived and, as one says in cruel stories, died. She consoled her and restored her to the imagination of our own days through a laceration of oblivion, that eternal gesture against death.[3]

If Rossana saw in her 'the ancient return to the mother' capable of repelling death and oblivion, I could do no less than associate her with an exalted vision of pain: the *Pietà* that embraces a crucified Christ. Her response to this reading (one that seemed, not mistakenly, to contain a judgement)—'You are wrong!'—came immediately, when I asked her to continue our dialogue in the journal founded in the same year, 1987—a journal which I founded and then directed for the following decade.

---

3 Rossanda, *Anche per me*, p. 208.

Rossana put the relation to the other (man, his universe, his 'public commandments') at the centre, which does not necessarily entail dependence or martyrdom. In her own experience at least, this meant recognizing oneself as 'a female unit in a plenum of male and female units'—a plant that grows in the earth of the other, from whom to discover similarities and differences, with whom to converse and conflict, to understand, allowing oneself to be enchanted by all 'that which lives and surrounds us'. She emphasized that differences can be included and forgiven even in love: to embrace the unique in the other without searching for a fusion but also without denying the sweetness of the 'perception of the beating of another blood', of 'the hand that offers itself', of 'the words exchanged.'

Her gaze immediately returns to politics, just as it had 'fallen upon' her: the 'useless unfreedoms' of arrogance, power and the other, less visible kinds of violence that make some people the object of others' choices; inequalities intolerable to the degree they could be avoided. Her fear that the form of autonomy espoused by feminism might be a way of folding back into the self led her to claim that, putting saviour tendencies aside, embracing the world was also a form of love: seeing the world as your own, passing through history, never looking back, choosing where and how to intervene.

It was clear that, while I was discovering the hidden, profound predeterminations of the dominion of one sex over another, for Rossana the horizon on which freedom could be constructed—including her liberty 'as a woman'—remained in the 'time which has been given to us', about which she wants to know everything, including the day of her own death. For her, that human terminus—the discovery that we are 'concluded in time just as much as in the extension of our minds'—was simply tragic and irresolvable.

Her conversation with me and with those questions that came to her through feminism was reprised in a more pressing and, in some ways, more heartfelt manner in *Lapis* 7 (1990), taking inspiration from her reading of Giovanna Grignaffini's essay on Chabrol's film *Story of Women*. Rossana was surprised at how Giovanna had put the hands of the protagonist—played by Isabelle Huppert—at the centre of her account: 'exiled, impoverished hands, hands that work and perform abortions.' The historical context—the war, the German occupation—were left out of the frame, deemed less relevant, as if a woman could be thought of as 'extraneous' to a history that simply crushed her and made her into a scapegoat.

In her attempt to uncover the great paradigms of male ideology (within which women were trapped), women's time returned to mark the differences and attempts at proximity between us, not without a veiled

allusion to the fact that we were speaking from distinc-
tively different experiences and places: I from my summer on the island of Carloforte, she from Paris, 'in that
strange kind of Carloforte a big metropolis can become
if you do not usually live or work there, or know it well;
you feel alone, as if standing before the sea' (54).

I had already considered the matter of 'women's
temporality' with some discomfort when it was
proposed to me not as an 'obligatory journey'
but a 'positively different' experience. What's
more, Lea's columns have often encouraged me
to flatten out days, locations and their happenings, to reduce them to a low and fleeting hum,
a distraction from the long time-periods and
firmer ground of self-knowledge—a knowledge
like an excavation that constantly expands across
the same ground, with the same tools [. . .]
in the same way that an archaeologist explores
an area containing treasures and artefacts [. . .].
Sometimes I think that, if I had to depict myself
and Lea, I would paint her intent on lifting up
with her hands the find that refracts consciousness of the world and of the self, while I would
draw myself all out of focus running without
pause towards some moving horizon, looking
behind me and swerving as I press ahead,
questioning unstable worlds—those of life and

death—in all their diversity, while time passes, or rather flies by. (50)

In the solitude of her Paris, as if in front of the 'great greys of winter' (54), Rossana would have wanted to find the thoughts and words that might bring women together, if it were not for the intervention of an event of enormous political importance, one that opened up a fracture between 'depths and history', a fracture that could not be easily recomposed. It was 1989 and the fragmentation of the communist regimes—the fall of a doctrine of which, in one way, she considered herself also a victim—exposed her yet again to the criticism of having sacrificed her life to a 'guilty mistake'. The same women who looked upon her role as the 'androgynous friend' (56) with affection, able to move between opposite poles, did not seem to be aware of how deep and painful—almost schizophrenic—it was to need to 'divide oneself in two'. For her this meant finding the connections between liberation from a dominion that had marked the most intimate events (the body, sexuality, motherhood) and a social, economic and political system, both based on the laws of money and inequality.

'I am not two'—Rossana concluded—'I am only one' (60).

And beyond her devilish 'totalizing manias' (59), Rossana demonstrated that she could also be 'integral' in her few but extremely lucid articles for *Lapis*.

As far as I'm concerned, the social manifestation of the division of the sexes and the theoretical problem to which it leads me is more than enough: how the current class contradictions overlap and separate, as well as the contradictions of unequal powers in economics and politics—and then there is another contradiction that passes through capitalism and its forms, through culture and its forms, refining and vanishing: the contradiction between male and female. Without doubt there is an overlap, in the active sense of exchange and reinforcement, and there is certainly also a separation, and I will try to explain this very quickly, because I fear it is this very lattice that holds my interventions together.[4]

Despite some misunderstandings—such as my criticism of sexual dualism and that search for connections that Rossana sometimes mistakes for fusion—our friendship would never have been so steadfast had it not been for our mutual criticism of a certain essentialist tendency within feminism. As she wrote in the first article, one cannot free oneself by praising difference or believing that patriarchal dominion cancelled out an originary, female substance that now needs to be

---

4 Rossanda, *Anche per me*, p. 21.

brought out. We similarly agreed on the fact that there does not exist a knowledge bound to a 'particular perception of the body, a knowledge that women would possess more than men' (63), due to their generative capacity: identifying with the body, destined to take care of it and participate in its imaginative exaltation and historical insignificance, all the while being a body to which others have provided names and forms.

The knowledge of the body—Rossana writes—is in reality 'a perception', a 'model of the body', one exterior to immediate experience and tending to become an experience in itself. This is not 'knowledge' but a dense and 'dramatic "fantasy"' (64). Symbolic coercion, identities, and 'gender' roles are considered 'natural' for both men and women, but it is women above all—as Rossana emphasizes—who have been defined by their appearance, through their being first and foremost seen, and by external functions like maternity and seduction.

For both myself and Rossana, the foundation of this 'cultural membrane'—'two plates of armour' overlapping other bans connected to awareness of the body—seems to be so deep, so primordial and dramatic that it has unconsciously marked the destiny of the majority of women for centuries.

A mirror constantly accompanies her: man's staring at her body, for whom she is first and foremost either beautiful or ugly, blonde or brunette, legs and breasts and waists. She cannot but see herself seen. Women who behave as if this were not the case are deemed frigid, self-deniers. And they are few and far between. We are so accustomed to caring for our appearance that it seems eccentric to not do so [. . .]. One can spend an entire life without perceiving anything other than this fabric of received images, stratified and interwoven with direct but hidden perceptions—all while 'caring for oneself' and for others. But it is a slim basis for 'knowledge'. (72)

For *Lapis*, Rossana wrote on women's dependence on an unattainable model of perfection, before which they must feel perennially inadequate but which at the same time provides an attractive image that might render them powerful, desired of feared by the other sex. These pages were striking for their courageous exposure of the self—the relation to the body, ageing, death—and for the lucidity of a kind of analysis that was at the centre of feminist practice in those years.

In particular, not having experienced maternity, it was on beauty (a gift that has been recognized in her more by others than by herself) that her focus fell, an attention that is at times cold and clinical, at others friendly and humorous. This was a topic that was difficult, elusive and embarrassing to the extent that it remained taboo even for those feminists who practised consciousness-raising and the analysis of the subconscious, a fact confirmed by the editors of *Lapis* when we searched for someone who might write about it.

With a freedom for which I have never stopped envying her, in the two articles explicitly on the body—'On the Threshold of Mystery' and 'This Body That Inhabits Me'—Rossana managed to speak about the *unpresentable* character of the uncomfortable and, at times, dramatic concreteness with which women have been compelled to measure themselves by their attractiveness, their physical and erotic desirability, forced to recognize that they would never be as they should or might want to be, and thus always lacking in comparison to the divas of cinematic imagination and, above all, resigned in horror to the wounds of ageing.

I once heard Catherine Deneuve respond to the question: 'How does a very beautiful woman live?' with the words: 'She looks in the mirror every morning to spot where the cracks are starting to appear.' As for me, given that I didn't like myself, I was always suspicious—there was always a crack, which meant I was not particularly disturbed by the onset of ageing. I used to examine myself coldly, with a friendly glance: waist, chest, hips, the lines of my arms and legs. They were blurring—this much was clear [. . .]. The body ages downwards. This is the moment in which the 'form', however modest it may already have been, moves on.

But to encounter Rossana in the originality of her political and personal journey—the insistence on communicating with the other, even in their difference, her desire to change everything, the impossibility resigning herself in front of every form of predetermination—one needs to return to the titles of those two essays and what she considers the most painful and tragic aspect of the human condition.

In *Anche per me* she had written:

It might be difficult, but it is nonetheless wise to recognize that the human condition—caught in a balance between life and death, this biological, ahistorical fact, the indestructible residue of the individuality of suffering—is the dark edge which political emancipation meets at the limit of its journey. The form and mission of this emancipation does not lie in restoring humankind to happiness but only (only!) in freeing it from the intolerability of injustice.[5]

Perhaps it is only a woman who can have a relation to the body—her own, the body of those she loves—that allows her to love it as a whole and not to conceal it in its decay, almost as though this were not 'sayable' [. . .] But in order

---

5 Rossanda, *Anche per me*, p. 30.

to violate this ban one has to know how to love the concrete. A different perception of the person is required, as well as of matter and consciousness, memory and oblivion, the ludic and the obscure, words that flow and those that get stuck, movements that melt and those that are frozen.[6]

Entirely aware of the many 'unfreedoms' and injustices created by the historical relation of power between sexes and between classes—intolerable because they could be fought and removed—Rossana nevertheless respects the immutable power the body has over all humankind, not only due to its material finitude but also in the primordial ban by which we remain at the borders of its mystery and obscurity:

While being the closest, the body is also the least frequented zone of understanding. To explain why, one must turn to psychoanalysis and modern psychiatry. I will limit myself here to claiming that knowledge of the body, even though it logically ought to be the first and most interesting object of exploration, has always been quasi-magically off-limits. The body is born, grows old and dies and we are born, grow old and die with it: *with*, as if it were something other than ourselves. Raise

6 Rossanda, *Anche per me*, p. 117.

your hands, all those who would not have spoken in this way. (67)

If men and women have different perceptions of
the body due to the domination through which one sex
enslaved the other and imposed its vision of the world,
it is nevertheless 'tragic' for both to realize that, sooner
or later: 'It is going. I am not' (91).

Leaving dualism behind and finding connections
did not mean annulling the tension that passes between
biology and history, between insuperable limits and
those situations that one can change.

I must recognize that only in recent years, and after
a sudden illness—brief but which carried the risk of
death—have I understood that Rossana was right to
admonish me for insistently invoking the body without
knowing anything about it. Or, rather, I spoke about it
in its psychoanalytic sense—drives, feelings, dreams,
etc.—but I lacked any direct 'inquisitive' perception of
the living body in all its material concreteness. Rossana
referred to this 'unfreedom' that evades all forms of
political activity, by speaking of resignation and horror,
but again employing her tone of 'friendly irony':

The day the body will send me a message to
say: 'Listen, I'm tired, enough now', I hope it
will give me time to reply: 'OK. And thank you,
I've enjoyed myself greatly.' (95)

There are two other essays which, even if not explicitly autobiographical, are nevertheless no less revealing of the questions that feminism posed to her 'person'.

Being a woman who had acted within an area that was 'masculine par excellence', fighting against that which seemed unjust to her but without considering men as the enemy, who had thought of herself as a 'piece of the world's mosaic', and who hesitated to give priority to her belonging to a sex, she appeared to feminism as a 'one-off' or, as she said of herself, 'a combatant who was as scruffy as she was headstrong.'

Figures of female 'warriors'—passed down through history or legend as having lived for a large part of their lives dressed as men, soldiering like Nadezhda Durova ('A Hussar Called Hope'), or as political revolutionaries, like Théroigne de Méricourt—could not but solicit Rossana's interest and lead her to the problematic terrain of the relation between sex and gender, between the fate that deprives women of freedom over their bodies and public speech, and the 'cunning' by which some have sought a way out from this destiny. '[S]exual transvestism [. . .] does not imply the refusal of an identity' (21), Rossana writes, but in Durova's case it was instead a way to remove herself from the destructive unhappiness of her mother, an unhappiness from which she had been rejected but which then forced into a similarly unhappy alternative.

A hussar in the Russian campaign against Napoleon, at the end of the war Durova returned to being 'a woman within society', received 'with great applause' but looked upon with suspicion 'as someone who did not belong to one sex or the other' (25). When herself wrote, she realized that this was not an available path, and instead 'a different status' for women needed to be conquered. Of particular interest is Rossana's comment in which she makes it clear that this is not only an issue of emancipation:

> The book emphasizes how this different status does not just imply the power to have other ambitions [. . .]. Rather, it means living free from one's body and freely choosing a discipline that is not imposed by the patriarchy. Even military discipline is preferable, because much is asked and expected of the 'noble', and to a great extent the discipline is open to a wide range of self-realizations. (33)

In Rossana's description of Durova, she attempts to see aspects of what, to an external view, might appear as her androgyny. In reality what emerges here, even more than elsewhere, even if by proxy, is the exceptionality of her experience: the solidity, sense of duty and compassion that Nadezhda demonstrated in war are gifts not extraneous to her, just as the refusal of the unhappiness and horrendous mutilation that women have suffered were not extraneous either: an unhappy sex, 'denied by and to itself' (35). Through Nadezhda, Rossana could claim that 'making oneself a man' could be seen as a method for living differently in the world, for allowing oneself ways of living otherwise not allowed to one's sex.

Théroigne de Méricourt seems even closer on account of the political passion that in 1789 would bring her, at only thirty years of age, to attend the Estates General, give public speeches and found revolutionary clubs. She is a figure who feminist historians themselves have seemed to confine to the transvestism of the 'beautiful warrioress' or 'the soldier'. For Rossana, Théroigne—dressed as an Amazon, armed with pistol and sabre—again symbolized the will to be 'other', to share and produce ideas, to open up the road to a female protagonism that acts politically and thus represents a threat to the worldly government of men. In the figure of this small, ill, restless woman whose political passion was exposed to misogyny on both right and left right—up until a depressive psychosis brought her to end her days in the Salpetrière—Rossana saw a sign of what it meant for a woman to enter into the public sphere, and the contradictions towards which the feminism of the 1970s was heading.

> In the end, it's as if there were two different mental processes taking place that could not overlap: on the one hand, a reflection on their own sex, forever excluded from politics; on the

other, a reflection on the opening up of political society (one that *still* excluded them) in the context of an unprecedented situation in which new relations, as well as new forms of power and dependence were being forged. The historically immediate—the concrete formation of the Revolution through the transformation of choices and values—was so alien and unusual for them that they could not truly embrace it, could not truly intervene, truly choose. (45)

In his 1967 article 'Don Milani and the Schoolboys of Barbiana', Elvio Fachinelli had already focused on how difficult it was to superimpose the two enigmas of history—economic exploitation and the body, sexuality—how the 'individual repression of the social' and the 'social repression of individuals' had long remained in parallel.[7] The search for the connections and activity that might avoid traditional dualisms was made even more complicated by the intervention of the feminist revolution in the middle of the twentieth century, one that yet again brought to light the false nature of the sexual division of labour and the constructions of gender: a particularity that the class-based Left (whether parliamentary or otherwise) considered

---

7 Elvio Fachinelli, 'Don Milani e i ragazzi di Barbiana', *Quaderni piacentini* 31 (1967): 271–5; reprinted as 'Un testo cinese' in *Al cuore delle cose. Scritti politici, 1967–1989* (Dario Borso ed.) (Rome: DeriveApprodi, 2016), pp. 21–6.

as merely superstructural and thus subordinate to the overturning of economic and political relations of power.

For Rossana—who due to her personal history found herself involved on both sides—impatience, doubts and calls for help were understandable. Given the conflictual character of the times, I'm not surprised on re-reading her today that it was she herself who, taking a cue from her own biography, focused on how the 'murky imaginary transmitted by history', 'shadows' and 'phantasmatic projection' (38) that has covered over the reality of women, were also not alien to feminist historians themselves.

> The abyss between imagination and reality was immense [. . .]. It is worth reflecting on the impossibility of recording the reality of the women who emerged in those years, and the concurrent creation of deformed figures, whether through adoration or enmity. This impossibility resounds with the fear of the irruption of a sex that is not only moved, as one says, by basic needs—such as the bread that Paris so cruelly lacked—but, when this is the case, goes out and does politics, becoming a new protagonist.

Rossana's rare, precious writings for *Lapis*, for which I remain truly grateful, thus also represent a lucid, Luciferian revolt against the mystifications of a history that continues to hand down only 'legendary relics, whether of valour or horror' (46) as far as the female world is concerned, proving Virginia Woolf right: imaginatively of the highest importance, historically insignificant.[8]

Liberation from a form of domination that marks all institutions but is also inscribed into the 'obscurity of bodies'[9] requires long arcs of time and I must admit that, from this viewpoint, Rossana's melancholy is unfortunately well founded.

---

8 Melandri paraphrases Virginia Woolf, *A Room of One's Own* (London: Hogarth, 1935), p. 66. [Trans.]

9 Pierre Bourdieu, *Masculine Domination* (Richard Nice trans.) (Stanford: Stanford University Press 1998), p. 81.

INDEX OF NAMES

Aleramo, Sibilla (Maria Felicina Faccio) 49

Alexander I of Russia (Alexander Pavlovich Romanov) 24

Badinter, Élisabeth 38

Barnave, Antoine-Pierre-Joseph-Marie 42

Beaton, Cecil 65

Bourdieu, Pierre 120n28

Buttafuoco, Annarita 36

Buxtehowen, Friedrich Wilhelm von 25

Campagnano, Lidia 51

Chabrol, Claude 47, 104

Chevalier d'Éon 23

Christie, Agatha 92

Corday, Charlotte (Marie-Anne-Charlotte de Corday d'Armont) 37

Cukor, George 65

de Condorcet, Nicolas (Marie-Jean-Antoine-Nicolas de Caritat de Condorcet) 37, 45

de Gouges, Olympe (Marie Gouze) 36, 37, 39, 40, 43, 44

de Méricourt, Théroigne (Anne-Joseph Ter-wagne) 36–46, 114, 116

Deneuve, Catherine (Catherine Fabienne Dorléac) 89, 110

Dostoevsky, Fyodor Mikhailovich 13

Durov, Vasily 29
Durova, Nadezhda A. 23–35, 114–15

Esquirol, Jean-Étienne-Dominique 41

Fachinelli, Elvio 117, 118n24
Fraire, Emanuela 98
Frazer, James 62
Freud, Sigmund 49, 73

Gabriel, Georges-François-Marie 42,
Garbo, Greta (Greta Lovisa Gustafsson) 64–5, 86
Gargani, Aldo 62n2
Ginzburg, Carlo 62
Ginzburg, Natalia 64
Giorgi, Stefania 72n8
Grignaffini, Giovanna 47, 48, 104

Hawthorne, Nathaniel 87
Hays Code (named after William H. Hays) 66

Hayworth, Rita (Margarita Carmen Cansino) 66
Heidegger, Martin 56
Hepburn, Katharine 66
Huppert, Isabelle 47, 48, 104

Joan of Arc 22
Joseph II of Habsburg-Lorraine 44

Kafka, Franz 13, 19,
Kautsky, Lulu (Luise Ronsperger Kautsky) 102

Lacombe, Claire 37, 39
Léon, Pauline 37, 39
Lubitsch, Ernst 64
Luxemburg, Rosa 101

Mann, Thomas 88
Mantegazza, Paolo 49
Marat, Jean-Paul 37, 41
Marie Antoinette of Habsburg-Lorraine 36, 37, 40, 44
Melandri, Lea 1n2, 4n4, 13n7, 16n8, 54n5

Melville, Herman 13
Michelet, Jules 36
Monroe, Marilyn 64

Napoleon (Bonaparte) 24, 115

Pera, Pia 24n4, 34
Pinel, Philippe 41
Pushkin, Alexander Ser-geyevich 25

Robespierre, Maximilien-François-Isidore de 43
Roland, Manon (Manon Philipon, later Marie-Jeanne Roland de la Platière) 36, 37, 39
Romme, Gilbert 42
Rossanda, Mimma 84, 87
Roudinesco, Élisabeth 38

Sacks, Oliver 74n9
Saint-Just, Louis-Antoine de 43
Schiffer, Claudia 87
Shakespeare, William 22, 32

Shorter, Edward 63n4
Sieyès, Emmanuel-Joseph 42
Stanwyck, Barbara (Ruby Catherine Stevens) 66
Stein, Gertrude 18
Suleau, François-Louis 40
Suvorov, Alexander Vasi-lyevich 25

Tatafiore, Roberta 72n8
Trota of Salerno 61

Verrocchio, Andrea del (Andrea di Michele di Francesco Cione)
von Kleist, Heinrich 23
von Trotta, Margarethe 101

Walker, Alexander 64n6
Wittgenstein, Ludwig 62
Woolf, Virginia 119

Yimou, Zhang 75, 78–9, 80